WAR STORIES FROM CAPITOL HILL

Real Politics in America

Series Editor: Paul S. Herrnson, *University of Maryland*

The books in this series bridge the gap between academic scholarship and the popular demand for knowledge about politics. They illustrate empirically supported generalizations from original research and the academic literature using examples taken from the legislative process, executive branch decision making, court rulings, lobbying efforts, election campaigns, political movements, and other areas of American politics. The goal of the series is to convey the best contemporary political science research has to offer in ways that will engage individuals who want to know about real politics in America.

WAR STORIES FROM CAPITOL HILL

EDITED BY

Colton C. Campbell
Florida International University

Paul S. Herrnson
University of Maryland

UPPER SADDLE RIVER, NEW JERSEY 07458

Library of Congress Cataloging-in-Publication Data

War stories from Capitol Hill/edited by Colton C. Campbell, Paul S. Herrnson.
   p. cm.—(Real politics in America)
Includes bibliographical references and index.
  ISBN 0-13-028088-7
  1. United States. Congress.   2. United States—Politics and government.
I. Campbell, Colton C.   II. Herrnson, Paul S.   III. Series.
  JK1021.W37   2004
    328.73—dc22

                        2003015485

Editorial Director: Charlyce Jones Owen
Acquisitions Editor: Glenn Johnston
Assistant Editor: John Ragozzine
Editorial Assistant: Suzanne Remore
Director of Marketing: Beth Mejia
Marketing Assistant: Jennifer Bryant
Prepress and Manufacturing Buyer: Sherry Lewis
Interior Design: John P. Mazzola
Cover Design: Kiwi Design
Cover Photo: Craig Arness/Corbis
Composition/Full-Service Project Management: Kari C. Mazzola and John P. Mazzola
Printer/Binder: RR Donnelley & Sons Company
Cover Printer: Phoenix Color Corp.

This book was set in 10/12 Palatino.

Real Politics in America
Series Editor: Paul S. Herrnson

Pearson Education LTD.
Pearson Education Singapore, Pte. Ltd
Pearson Education, Canada, Ltd
Pearson Education–Japan
Pearson Education Australia PTY, Limited

Pearson Education North Asia Ltd
Pearson Educación de Mexico, S.A. de C.V.
Pearson Education Malaysia, Pte. Ltd
Pearson Education, Upper Saddle River, NJ

10 9 8 7 6 5 4 3 2 1
ISBN 0-13-028088-7

*In recognition of the American Political Science Association
Congressional Fellowship Program,
which for more than half a century has enabled scholars
to temporarily abandon the Ivory Tower
to experience life on Capitol Hill*

Contents

PREFACE

War Stories from Capitol Hill presents insiders' accounts of how Congress works. It covers the parliamentary maneuvers, plots, counterplots, lively debates, triumphs, and dedication involved in making something happen on Capitol Hill. It includes a collection of original essays written by individuals who have worked for the U.S. House of Representatives or the U.S. Senate, and who are familiar with the personalities, conflict, compromise, creativity, and persistence that embody congressional politics. The essays illustrate the enduring topics essential to understanding Capitol Hill. Each essay focuses on one or more aspects of congressional controversy experienced by the writer, and places the "story" in a broader historical and conceptual framework necessary for understanding how Congress and its members function. The chapters tie the authors' insightful first-person experiences with the ins and outs of everyday legislative life to broader themes of congressional politics. Some essays combine quantitative data analysis with descriptions and examples drawn from real politics, as is consistent with the style of other books written for the *Real Politics in America* series.

Contemporary political science scholarship lays a firm foundation for comprehending how the institution of Congress operates and why lawmakers reach the decisions they do, but it could be more successful in presenting this information to students and the general public. Results generated from formal models, statistical analyses, case studies, and systematic comparisons—the basic tools of the discipline—are not always accessible to practitioners or the general reader. In Congress, it is not always possible to construct a purely rational decision-making process for any but the simplest, lowest-level decisions. What makes the legislative process so hard to simplify is that there is often an elaborate maze of subtleties to be sorted out and disparate goals to be weighed. A perspective that reduces congressional structure and decision making solely to the calculation of optimal means may disregard much of the political process in Congress. There are occasions when lawmaking involves networks of personal relationships among actors with a range of goals and motives, behind-the-scenes maneuvering and informal arrangements, and accumulated practice that is not always captured by rigid theoretical frameworks. Often the best way to start examining Congress and its operations is to recognize former House Speaker Thomas P. "Tip" O'Neill's insight: Politics is an art. In short, real politics matters.

The chapters that follow bridge the gap between academic scholarship and the popular demand for knowledge about politics. Our goal is to provide readers with a manageable perspective on the workings of Congress and real-life American politics, enhancing their ability to make the connections between the theory and practice of politics. Our hope is to illustrate empirically supported generalizations from original research and the academic literature, using examples taken from the legislative process. The decisions of individuals who work in government or who seek to get elected or appointed to public office can have tremendous consequences for Americans and citizens of other nations. The same is true of the efforts of party leaders, interest group lobbyists, voters, and protesters who try to influence the actions of those in government.

This book could not have been completed without the assistance of many individuals and organizations. First and foremost we must thank our authors. They tolerated our exhortations to put aside the "rules" of writing they learned in graduate school, to make their chapters interesting and accessible to a broad audience, and to give readers a sense of what it is like to participate in real politics. Next, we wish to thank Beth Mejia, Jessica Drew, and Heather Shelstadt of Prentice Hall, and Kari Callaghan Mazzola, who contributed to the book's clarity with her careful editorial and production supervision. We also thank the following reviewers for their helpful feedback: John H. Aldrich, Duke University; William T. Bianco, Penn State; Lawrence C. Dodd, University of Florida; C. Lawrence Evans, The College of William & Mary; Morris P. Fiorina, Stanford University; Representative David E. Price, U.S. House of Representatives; and Charles Stewart III, Massachusetts Institute of Technology. We also want to acknowledge the American Political Science Association Congressional Fellowship Program. The program gave most of the book's contributors the opportunity to work in Congress and observe firsthand how it operates. Finally, we wish to thank the members of Congress who employed us. The relationship that exists between elected politicians and the political aides, fellows, and interns who staff their offices is a remarkable one. Members rely on their staffs to help them cope with the immense workload that Congress imposes on them. In so doing, they surrender some of the control they have over their own political futures and give their aides the opportunity to participate in deliberations that could fundamentally alter the lives of millions of people living in the United States and abroad. All of the participants in this book are indebted to the members whom we served. They had enough faith in us to allow us to participate in the legislative process and observe firsthand how Congress really works.

Colton C. Campbell

Paul S. Herrnson

ABOUT THE CONTRIBUTORS

CHRISTOPHER J. BAILEY is author of *Congress and Air Pollution: Environmental Policies in the USA* and *The Republican Party in the U.S. Senate, 1974–84: Party Change and Institutional Development*, and coeditor of *Developments in American Politics 3*. He served as an APSA congressional fellow in the office of Senator Harry Reid (D-Nev.).

JEFFREY R. BIGGS is director of the APSA Congressional Fellowship Program. He is coauthor of *Honor in the House: Speaker Tom Foley*. He served as an APSA congressional fellow and later as communications director in the Office of the House Speaker, Thomas Foley (D-Wash.).

THOMAS L. BRUNELL is assistant professor of political science at Northern Arizona University. His articles appear in the *American Political Science Review, American Journal of Political Science, Journal of Politics*, and *Legislative Studies Quarterly*. He served as an APSA congressional fellow in the House Subcommittee on the Census.

COLTON C. CAMPBELL is associate professor of political science at Florida International University. He is author of *Discharging Congress: Government by Commission*, coauthor of *Impeaching Clinton: Partisan Strife on Capitol Hill*, and coeditor of numerous books, most recently *Congress and the Internet*. He served as an APSA congressional fellow in the office of Senator Bob Graham (D-Fla.).

PAUL S. HERRNSON is director of the Center for American Politics and Citizenship and professor of government and politics at the University of Maryland. He is author of *Congressional Elections: Campaigning at Home and in Washington* and *Party Campaigning in the 1980s*, as well as editor and coeditor of numerous books, including *Playing Hardball: Campaigning for the U.S. Congress; After the Revolution: PACs, Lobbies, and the Republican Congress*; and *Responsible Partisanship? The Evolution of American Political Parties since 1950*. He served as an APSA Steiger congressional fellow in the office of Representative David E. Price (D-N.C.).

DAVID L. LEAL is assistant professor of political science at the University of Texas at Austin. He has conducted research on campaigns and elections, Hispanic politics, and Congress. He has published articles in journals such as *British Journal of Political Science, American Politics Quarterly, Political Behavior, Social Science Quarterly, Urban Affairs Review, Policy Studies Journal*, and *Hispanic Journal of Behavioral Sciences*. He served as an APSA Steiger congressional fellow in the office of Senator John F. Kerry (D-Mass.).

KELLY D. PATTERSON is chairman and associate professor of political science at Brigham Young University. He is author of *Political Parties and the Maintenance of Liberal Democracy*, and coeditor of *Contemplating the People's Branch: Legislative Dynamics in the Twenty-First Century*. He has published articles in journals such as *Public Opinion Quarterly, Political Behavior, Polity, Presidential Studies Quarterly*, and *American Behavioral Scientist*. He served as an APSA congressional fellow in the office of Representative David E. Price (D-N.C.).

NICOL C. RAE is professor of political science at Florida International University. He is author of *The Decline and Fall of the Liberal Republicans: From 1952 to the Present; Southern Democrats*; and *Conservative Reformers: The Republican Freshmen and the Lessons of the 104th Congress*; coauthor of *Governing America: History, Culture, Institutions, Organization, Policy* and *Impeaching Clinton: Partisan Strife on Capitol Hill*; and coeditor of several books, most recently *Congress and the Politics of Foreign Policy*. He served as an APSA congressional fellow in the offices of Senator Thad Cochran (R-Miss.) and Representative George P. Radanovich (R-Calif.).

WAR STORIES FROM CAPITOL HILL

INTRODUCTION

GOVERNMENT IS NOT PHYSICS AND CONGRESS IS NOT A SUPERCOMPUTER

COLTON C. CAMPBELL AND PAUL S. HERRNSON

"A physics exercise, if done correctly, will yield similar results every time," said Senator Bob Graham (D-Fla.) to a classroom of college students. "But government involves people, with different ideas, which produces inconsistencies and unpredictability."[1] One thing is certain about Congress: The institution never lacks for variety. Steeped in tradition and rich in controversy, Congress embodies the collection of individuals who serve in it at any given time, whose personal motives, goals, and talents have a direct impact on how the institution operates. Only Congress can pass bills that create new federal programs, alter the tax code, or appropriate federal dollars for important—and not so important—national projects. Whether it does these things depends in large part on the efforts of both legislators and their staffs, and how well they overcome differences of opinion and work together.

CONGRESS, THE CONSTITUTION, AND CONFLICT

The framers of the Constitution deliberately intended to introduce division and disharmony in government. The individuals who serve in Congress, the presidency, and the courts represent different constituencies, are empowered for different lengths of service, and are responsible for carrying out different enumerated activities. The system further disperses power because it has many points of access that different groups can use to influence the federal government. The House and Senate, with their multitudes of committees, subcommittees, task forces, public hearings, and floor debates, provide what is perhaps the world's most open and most heavily scrutinized arena of conflict management and consensus building. When members of Congress and their

1

aides respond to the demands of their constituents, interest group representatives, members of the executive branch, or others who choose to petition the government, conflict invariably results.[2] Moving from conflict to compromise is essential to legislative success.

The Constitution dictates a special relationship between Congress and the presidency. Presidential appointees to the federal judiciary and the executive branch must be approved with the "advice and consent" of the Senate. Two-thirds of the Senate must approve all treaties that are negotiated by the president. Legislation is debated and approved on the House and Senate floors, but the president is involved in developing legislation and in rallying legislative support for it. Of course, if Congress passes a bill that meets with the president's disapproval, he can always veto it. Moreover, the United States cannot declare wars, form alliances, agree to strategic arms control accords, or make international trade agreements without the explicit approval of Congress.

CONGRESSIONAL LIFE AT HOME

Congress and its members perform two overlapping and sometimes conflicting functions: representation and lawmaking.[3] Congress, the representative institution, is local in its focus. This body is an assemblage of 535 unique individuals, each of whom has a unique set of values, goals, and constituents: the river boat captain and the professor of economics, the twenty-eight-year-old and the ninety-eight-year-old, the former welfare recipient and the self-made multimillionaire, the freshman and the fifteen-term veteran. Its members are primarily concerned with promoting the interests of their states and districts, providing constituent services, and educating voters about the Washington demands of their jobs. The electoral fortunes of these locally elected officials depend less upon what Congress produces as an institution than upon the support and goodwill of constituents who vote for them and contribute to their campaigns.[4] Lawmakers, therefore, take into serious consideration the preferences of voters in their districts, especially on issues that are visible to the public, responding to organized groups and claiming as much credit as possible for projects.[5] They fashion distinctive ways of projecting themselves and their records to their constituents in what one congressional observer calls their home style.[6] Once back home, the stereotypical southern legislator's drawl thickens, his khakis and a flannel shirt replace his tailored suits, and the Lincoln Town car he used in the capital is exchanged for a well-dented pickup truck. The quintessential congresswoman from the New York City area, on the other hand, may replace her conservative gray suit with an ensemble that is trendy and more colorful, but she is more likely to make her rounds in a taxi cab than a pickup truck, and the odds of her donning khakis and flannel are next to nil.

Although individual legislators do not necessarily mirror their constituents in terms of demographic characteristics, the recruitment process yields many who favor local views and prejudices. Contacts with voters throughout the campaign and while in office reinforce this convergence of views, as do representational norms adopted by most members.[7] Whatever the reason, voters believe their views are shared by their representatives. Members and their staffs devote constant attention and effort to dealing with "the folks back home." Simply put, constituency politics are ever present in the daily lives of senators and representatives. Former Representative Bud Shuster's (R-Pa.) passion for the decidedly passionless subject of asphalt and concrete easily illustrates the parochial connection lawmakers have with their district: As chairman of the House Transportation and Infrastructure Committee, he authorized money for the Bud Shuster Highway and Bud Shuster Byway in his district.[8]

Members make every effort to be seen in their home territory, regularly dashing from committee meetings to commute home for scheduled town meetings or open houses. The halls and committee rooms of Capitol Hill are virtual "no-man lands" before and after members leave the Hill for one of three area airports. Platoons of lobbyists retreat to their K Street offices in downtown Washington.

Assisting lawmakers in maintaining good relations with their constituents, as well as in attending to their duties in Washington, are young, well-educated, and often transient personal aides. Cramped in overcrowded office buildings like soldiers in a fox hole, these individuals perform a host of functions. They draft bills, write speeches, suggest policy initiatives, analyze bills, prepare position papers, and accompany members to committee hearings—and to the floor—where they locate references, suggest on-the-spot questions, and render other services. Members often have their legislative assistants attend committee hearings the member misses. State and district needs frequently influence staff composition. A senator from a farm state likely will employ at least one specialist in agricultural problems; an urban representative might hire a consumer affairs or housing expert; and Florida lawmakers often borrow NASA employees.[9]

Unlike the executive branch and much of American industry, Capitol Hill uses no achievement or personality tests, no personal counselors or career advisors to match a prospective congressional aide with a member of Congress who is a potential employer. Most aides are rarely defined by professional qualifications or specialized backgrounds. They are hired within a political context, and their stay on Capitol Hill is often limited to two or three years. As one report indicates, the members "hire them young, burn them out, and send them on."[10] House members may hire no more than eighteen full-time and four part-time employees. Senators' personal staffs range in size from thirteen to seventy-one because the Senate places no limits on the number of staff a senator may employ from their two personnel accounts. Senators from larger states receive more funds to hire personnel than do those from smaller ones. Nearly half of the personal staff who work for a member of the Senate are under thirty-five, and a sizeable majority of those in the House are under thirty. In a 1998 survey of 234 House and Senate staffers, a majority of aides on both sides of the aisle said it was no longer "rewarding and fun to work in Congress. And they expect to be gone within three years after starting their jobs."[11] Simply put, few are likely to be Capitol Hill lifers.

Each congressional office is its own enterprise. In most cases the organization, staff, and ergonomic design reflect the personality, interests, constituency, and politics of the individual legislator. Office interiors are a local Chamber of Commerce promoting the home state or district: Visitors to see Senator Bob Graham of Florida are greeted with a can of Florida orange juice; the office walls of Senator Max Baucus incorporate the side-paneling of an old Montana cabin; and Representative George Radanovich (R-Calif.), one of Congress's two vintners, displays his homegrown wines. Pictures romanticizing images of home adorn walls. Just about every office pays tribute to the legislative accomplishments of its member, where framed bills hang like championship pennants.

CONGRESSIONAL LIFE IN WASHINGTON

Congress, the lawmaking institution, is primarily national in its focus. It acts as a collegial body that drafts and approves legislation, oversees the bureaucracy, and holds hearings to learn about and publicize national concerns. This Congress is more than just a collection of its members. It is a mature institution that has an elaborate web of rules, structures, and traditions that mark the boundaries of the legislative playing field and thus limit an individual member's scope of action.[12] While this institutionalization enables Congress and its members to cope with a certain amount of contemporary change, it can also lead to organizational rigidity in which policy solutions are approached in small discrete steps, building policy and agreement from the bottom up. Lyndon B. Johnson likened this process to a bottle of bourbon: "If you take a glass at a time, it's fine" he said. "But if you drink the whole bottle in one evening, you have troubles."[13]

There are limits to what Congress can achieve through the give and take of the legislative process. Legislators are rarely equally concerned or equally knowledgeable about the issues that come before them. Disparate goals, interests, and constituent needs and concerns as well as unequal and scattered influence on Capitol Hill repeatedly stymie the legislative process. Members from agricultural districts and states are more likely to pay close attention to farm legislation than are members from urban areas, and members from urban areas are more likely to keep abreast of legislation that addresses the concerns of city dwellers than are their agrarian colleagues. On the Senate floor, in order to make a point about the need to help farmers, Senator Byron Dorgan (D-N.D.) decided to reveal that he had Cream of Wheat to start the day. And then he proceeded to explain how the dish was created: "Cream of Wheat, if you want to know the origin of it, just for fun—I notice the Presiding Officer is hanging on my every word here—came from Grand Forks, N.D., in the year 1893. A little old mill called the Diamond Mills was not doing very well. They had a scientist who was sort of moving around and trying to figure out what he could do with various parts of the grain. He used what are called the middlings of wheat, and he concocted what he called a 'breakfast porridge.'"[11] Dorgan's point was that Nabisco now owns the cereal and the company generates jobs in Minnesota, not for the farmers of North Dakota.

Congress readily displays the traits and biases of its membership and structure.[15] It is bicameral, with different electoral and procedural customs and many competing and informed agenda setters.[16] It is representative, particularly where geographic interests are concerned. Leadership and committees of both chambers attempt to control the legislative agenda, especially in the absence of unified party control of both the House and Senate, providing opportunities for obstruction.[17] Skilled committee leaders who prefer the status quo can use their prerogatives to water down, delay, or even derail a piece of legislation, as well as sermonize their political points. This competition naturally creates adversarial sources of information for legislators. Even under conditions of unified party control, differences in the rules under which lawmakers are elected may divide them on some issues.[18]

Legislative action is divided further by procedure and practice within each chamber of Congress. Leadership and its committees have the knowledge and incentive to serve as verifiers of the statements made by competing authorizing committees.[19] Members of the House minority party can use a range of tactics to undermine the majority's attempts to move legislation. For example, strategically worded amendments can be used to divide a bill's supporting coalition and, at least in the short term, dilatory tactics can be employed to slow down legislation. In short, the institution has become a place where, as one observer puts it, each member is a legislative broker.[20]

Another common hurdle to legislative success is that party leaders are reluctant to bring major legislation to the floor unless a comprehensive public relations campaign has been orchestrated and conducted on its behalf. Increasingly, House and Senate party leaders lead by going public.[21] These public relations battles require time, money, and other resources. Additionally, although members typically have well-formed preferences about the ends they hope a measure will produce, considerable uncertainty can exist over how to best achieve those ends. Proponents of an initiative need to search out policy and political information necessary to draft concrete legislative proposals and persuade colleagues that such proposals will indeed achieve the desired policy outcome—victory.[22] Disagreements about policy that characterize even relatively unified partisan majorities usually require concessions and logrolling if legislation is to move and party cohesion is to be maintained. Bringing off these transactions requires time, effort, cooperation, and other scarce political resources.[23]

RUNNING THE LEGISLATIVE GAUNTLET

The simple act of introducing or "dropping" a bill sets off a chain of events that may or may not lead to final passage. Most measures follow a path with various steps governed by rules, conventions, precedents, and folkways—unwritten norms of conduct that members are expected to observe.[24] The process is fairly predictable but the outcome is usually uncertain.[25] After Legislative Counsel has placed a legislative proposal in the proper legal phraseology and form to achieve congressional intent, a bill is introduced by a congressional sponsor and one or more cosponsors. The House Speaker or Senate presiding officer, advised by the chamber's parliamentarian, refers the proposal to the appropriate committee. In some cases sponsors are not serious; they act only to please some constituency or interest group. If they are serious, they will draft their own bill so as to raise the likelihood of its being referred to a friendly committee—often theirs—rather to an alternative, less friendly one. This strategic possibility exists because complex legislation and overlapping committee jurisdictions raise the chances of dividing the measure among more than one committee.

Once the bill goes to committee it is usually referred to an appropriate subcommittee by the committee chair. This is the first arena in which legislation is glimpsed in the light of day. Committees and subcommittees divide the thousands of bills introduced each year and assign them among smaller groups, allowing members to specialize and develop expertise in particular areas. They hold hearings, write legislation, advocate the passage of bills, and oversee their operation once they become law.[26]

If a bill is of sufficient importance, the subcommittee may set a date for public hearings, which have long been battlegrounds where contending forces seek to produce the public record needed to win the fight on the floor. Hearings can be tools used by the larger chamber to arrive at the common good, with the committee acting as the guardian of the general public interest after hearing from special-interest advocates who appear before it.[27] In this case the formal hearings take on features of a legislative court, where members verify the need for legislation in a particular policy area based upon the evidence of law and fact brought before them by interested parties.[28] Hearings may occasionally be vehicles used to further the interests of members. At times they may allow for the transmission of information from various interest groups to the committee, or be a propaganda platform for interest groups, with little thought given to a meaningful debate on the subject at hand. Hearings can also act as a safety valve, whereby group conflicts can be modified before they become explosive.

A certain amount of protocol must be observed at hearings. Members, arranged in a semicircular pattern around the committee chair according to party and seniority, with staff assistants seated behind them, listen to witnesses, maybe for a few hours or several days, sometimes for several months. Mounds of printed material lie before them: bills passed by the other chamber, with subcommittee-suggested changes; proposed measures; and thin green-colored volumes of the testimony taken at previous hearings. One of the important functions of any committee is reporting legislation to the home chamber. Designed to fully explain each measure approved by the committee, a "report" takes the form of a formal printed document and accompanies a bill as it goes to the House or Senate floor for action. It is also a reflection of the committee's interests—of the times in which they were written.

As the choreographed hearing unfolds, members make queries, solicit support, or interject opinions. The chair responds and, on occasion, looks to the ranking member for a nod of confirmation. Some members of the committee are circumspect in commenting. Others are bashful only for a time. During a hearing on international taxation, the late Democratic Senator Patrick Moynihan of New York, who sat on the Senate Finance Committee, chastised the CEO of a multinational corporation for a testimony in which the witnessed suggested that his American-based company might be better off operating in the Caymen Islands, rather than at home, in order to avoid double-taxation. "And do you expect the Marines to rescue you?" scolded the senator. "I suggest, sir, that you not come before the U.S. Senate and make that kind of declaration." After markup of the bill—revising it, adding and deleting sections, and preparing it for report to the full committee, assuming that a majority of committee members support it—the bill is ready to be scheduled for floor debate.

Throughout the hearing, assisting the subcommittee and committee members are the staff. A large amount of logistical responsibility is customarily delegated to the congressional aides servicing committees. In the high-pressure, overworked environment of the contemporary Congress, committee staffers turn the wheels of the committee system. They help party leaders shepherd bills on the floor of the Congress and participate in conference committee negotiations; they do policy research, arrange for witnesses (often stacking witness lists in favor of the position of the chair), compose and send to witnesses a questionnaire covering points on which their testimony is requested, prepare lists of questions for the members to ask in the hearings, and occasionally even ask the questions. In most cases, committees neither solicit nor receive complete information. Rather, they seek to promote certain views of their issues to bolster their abilities to produce favorable legislation.[29] A large part of the staff's jobs involves policy details, since they usually draft at least some amendments and bills as well as the committee reports that accompany bills to the floor. At various stages in the process of crafting and revising a bill, professional aides negotiate at the staff level with representatives of the affected agencies or interest groups to remove their objections.

Because their work is program- and agency-specific, and because their relationships with agencies are closer and endure longer than those of personal staff, professional committee staff tend to be better informed, more experienced, and more influential than personal staff. Typically, committee professional staff are older—16 percent are under thirty, another 24 percent are between thirty and thirty-nine, and the remaining 60 percent are forty years of age or older.[30] Many have worked in some other part of Capitol Hill prior to their appointment or have had extensive prior experience in various departments of the executive branch. A few come directly from private life, having had either direct or indirect contact with the lawmaker responsible for their appointment.

Assuming the Rules Committee in the House recommends a rule, and a motion or unanimous consent agreement is agreed to in the Senate or a motion to suspend the rule is made, members vote on the floor of their respective chamber to accept or reject the rule. Occupying the second and third stories of the House wing of the Capitol, the House chamber (139 feet long and 93 feet wide), the largest national parliamentary room in the world, offers a comfortable, theater-like setting, with rows of unmarked, stuffed leather seats, thick maroon carpeting, dark polished woodwork, and brass spittoons along the back railings. Five vertical aisles gently descend downward from the rear, dissect a semicircle of ten rows, and empty into the chamber's "well," the open area just below the Speaker's desk. On the left of the Speaker's desk is the portrait of Washington, on the right the portrait of Lafayette, both full-length. Below the raised dais of the Speaker sit clerks in two-tiered rows, numbering documents, recording entries into journals, and performing parliamentary tasks. Pages dressed in their traditional navy blue blazers, gray pants, red and blue ties, and white shirts dash between members and the Speaker's desk, carrying papers bearing motions, proposed amendments, notes from offices, and prepared speeches for entry into the *Congressional Record*.

Unlike the Senate, where senators have assigned chairs and desks, there are no desks in the House. Instead, members take almost any one they want of the 450 tan leather seats, built into sections from two to fifteen chairs, but with Republican majority members sitting on the east side of the middle dividing aisle to the right (facing) of the Speaker's rostrum, and Democrats sitting to the left of the Speaker. In the third row of both sides are two conference tables, where party leaders and committee members manage bills during floor debate.

Members behave differently on the House floor than in their offices. The floor and the cloakrooms just off it have a club-like atmosphere. As in most clubs, some members use the facilities to eat or doze off during quiet periods. There are the never-waste-a-minute members who always bring to the floor a stack of mail and memos to work on whenever the debates wane.[31] In contrast to the Senate, where spectators gawk at the quiet, casual, smaller scene below, searching for presidential contenders, House members stroll around in comparative anonymity.

After electronically casting their votes in the House (displayed on the walls behind and above the Speaker), and by the traditional roll call in the Senate, nonidentical bills must be meshed together into like form. Sometimes, with less controversial matters, one house will simply adopt the other's version as is. Sometimes the two chambers may send proposals or amendments back and forth—called "messaging"—to resolve points of difference. But for really important and controversial legislation, each chamber appoints conferees to participate in a conference committee.

In sum, before Americans feel the impact of a new government program it must run the legislative gauntlet four times (an authorization process in both the House and Senate and an appropriations process in both chambers), the House and Senate must agree on the results of each process, and the president must accept the agreements. Small wonder that of approximately twelve thousand bills introduced in each recent Congress, only about 600 ultimately become law, and even fewer are funded at the levels their proponents believed necessary.

CLASHING FORCES

Political parties, although not mentioned in the Constitution, are ubiquitous. They determine committee assignments, set the congressional agenda, influence roll call votes, and even dictate where representatives and senators sit in their respective chambers. Parties seek to maximize their influence on government through winning as many congressional seats (and other offices) as possible and centralizing power under their leaders. A party that controls many House seats and unites behind its leaders can have a tremendous impact on public policy. The Democrats demonstrated this when they restructured the role of the federal government in regulating the nation's economy during the New Deal, and when they redefined civil rights and social welfare policy during the 1960s.[32] Republican House members showed that they too could unite as a majority, when during the first 100 days following their takeover of the 104th Congress (1995–1997) they passed nine out of ten provisions of their much-celebrated Contract with America.[33]

After decades of entrenched partisan division, there has been a propensity for Democrats and Republicans in Congress to align themselves with their own interest groups' supporters, to protect and advance their interests.[34] Democrats have fixed themselves primarily in the social service and regulatory agencies of the domestic state; Republicans and their allies have sought to create a similar base in the military and national security apparatus, as well as with groups that actively promote business and family values.[35] Groups that participated in formulating the Contract with America were active in drafting specific legislative proposals.[36] Key lobbyists were seated with Republicans during certain formal hearings on issues of interest to their clients.

For instance, a lobbyist for a trade association used office space on Capitol Hill to work on strategy for the product liability bill.[37] In another well-publicized instance, the staff of the Senate Judiciary Committee was briefed by a lobbying firm representing electric utilities and other corporate interests subject to federal regulators before markup sessions on the Comprehensive Regulatory Reform Act.[38] By gathering these groups as well as grassroots groups together, Republicans ensured that each member of the alliance would contribute the highest level of effort.[39]

Because the parties often have policy-opposing goals and seek to wrest congressional seats from one another, they are the source of much of the conflict that takes place on Capitol Hill. Since the Republican's sweep of the House and Senate in 1994, new tactics and relationships have emerged. By the time members were seated, former Speaker Newt Gingrich and the new Republican majority not only submitted their battle plan, but also outlined a strategy for fulfilling that plan. In the early days of the "revolution," Majority Whip Tom "The Hammer" DeLay, a former exterminator who made a living killing fire ants and termites, was charged with ensuring that money flowed along the same stream as policy, that the probusiness deregulatory agenda of the House Republicans received the undivided financial support of the corporate interests that most benefited from them. His motto was an unabashedly blunt interpretation of the dicta of former Speaker Newt Gingrich: "If you want to play in our revolution, you have to live by our rules."[40] DeLay launched what came to be known as the "K Street Strategy," named for the downtown Washington avenue lined with lobbying headquarters, law firms, and trade associations. The strategy was to pressure those firms to remove Democrats from top jobs and replace them with Republicans.[41]

The initial order of business on Capitol Hill was to change the procedural environment in which Congress works. A frequent tactic of the Republican leadership in the 104th Congress was to bypass the committee system altogether. They used leadership-dominated committees, especially Budget and Rules, to shape legislation, or shifted from a committee-based system to an informal task force system that dealt with issues as disparate as gun control and political advocacy. Such temporary entities not only bypassed committees and their established issue networks, they allowed friendly groups greater access to the members while effectively shutting out others that did not agree with the Republicans.[42] Groups that Republican leaders considered their allies were able to come before them to argue their case out of public view. Further, because these task forces had no staff, their members were more inclined to rely on those interest groups for information and advice.

To further improve a bill's chances of passage, the GOP leadership attached a large number of substantive measures to appropriations bills. Stand-alone bills on such issues as abortion, workplace safety, and environmental regulation would be easier for President Clinton to veto than appropriations measures needed to keep the government running. Dubbed "Armey Proto-cols," Majority Leader Dick Armey (R-Texas) established a legislative strate-gy, authorizing committee chairmen to agree on policy legislation that would be pushed through the money bills.[43]

Republican procedural innovations significantly reduced congressional staffing by at least one-third, mainly by reducing the number of committee aides available to the minority-party Democrats. Further, committee chairs were granted control over the hiring of subcommittee staff with subcommit-tee chairmen and ranking minority members losing the authority to hire one aide each. Although committee staffs had come to be regarded as overblown and overactive, they provide vital services to members and have become in-tricately involved in shaping legislative outcomes. As legislation became more complex, congressional staff became more professional. Growing committee staffs also helped Congress oversee the huge and intimidating bureaucracy over the past several decades.[44]

The change from Democratic to Republican control of Congress dramat-ically altered which policy issues were pushed to the top of the legislative agenda and how such policies were processed, thus effecting the fortunes of different interest groups.[45] Groups not in tune with the Republican leader-ship's objectives were denied access to the legislative process. Like the De-mocrats who preceded them, the Republican leadership in the 104th Congress embraced organizations consistent with and committed to common objec-tives, adopting rules and practices that had the effect of enhancing the for-tunes of certain special interests and weakening the influence of others.[46] Conservative, pro-Republican groups—antitax, profamily, probusiness, an-tiabortion, and congressional reform organizations—were privy to the delib-erations of the Republican leadership; they worked with member and staff task forces drafting and developing legislation; they were invited to testify and participate in the markup of legislation; and the new majority encour-aged them to campaign actively for public support and passage of the Con-tract with America and subsequent GOP-sponsored legislation.[47] On taxes, for instance, the lobbying of the conservative coalition of interest groups helped ensure party unity behind the $500 per child tax credit.[48]

Conversely, groups that advocated liberal positions on social and moral issues, and that enjoyed preferred access when the Democrats were in con-trol, suddenly were fenced out. Members of organized labor, such as the American Federation of Labor-Congress of Industrial Organization (AFL-CIO) and the United Food and Commercial Workers International Union, for example, found themselves in a bunker because of direct attacks by the Re-publican leadership.[49] Prior to 1994, labor lobbying involved the direct so-licitation of members of Congress to sponsor or cosponsor legislation and persuading Democrats and moderate Republicans to support labor bills.[50] Perhaps the most visible sign of labor's fall from grace was the loss of ac-cess to the Doorkeeper's office, a windowless room centrally located in the

Capitol, in a suite of offices occupied by the Doorkeeper. Here, union lobbyists were entitled to make telephone calls and wait between meetings with legislators and their staff, an enviable outpost in a world where "access and information are prime commodities."[51]

FROM INKWELLS TO WIRELESS MODEMS

Contemporary lawmakers are hard-pressed to cope with their crowded schedules. When the first Congress convened, the United States had a tiny population, mostly rural and uneducated, with a simple social and industrial structure. Changes occurred slowly, and the government's tasks were few. Today's situation, however, is 180 degrees opposite. In the Capitol, elevator operators still greet members and visitors, paintings of powder-wigged founding fathers still gaze down from their gilded frames. Senate desks still have inkwells and goose-quill pens along with crystal sand shakers for blotting ink. Forty-eight of these desks date back to 1819 when they were purchased following the fire that badly damaged the Capitol and its furnishing, with several still bearing the knife-inscribed names of prior occupants. On the marble ledges flanking the president of the Senate's mahogany desk there are two Japanese lacquer snuffboxes, always kept filled, though their contents remain unused. But such traditions now share the corridors of power with fiber-optic cable links, PCs, cell phones, and wireless modems. Staffers can even order lunch from the House food system over the Internet at <www.specialordersdeli.com>.

In the midst of any congressional session, legislators can be seen shuttling between committee rooms to attend simultaneously occurring hearings and markups. "Today," reflected former Senator Nancy Landon Kassebaum (R-Kan.), "there's almost an information overload, a bombardment by news, by faxes. Everything is instantaneous with too little time for thoughtful reflection."[52] One longtime watcher of Congress summed up the hectic legislative life by observing:

> Legislators have very little time for reflection. There are demands upon their attention literally every minute of the day—and these demands would be made every minute of the night too if not for unlisted telephone numbers. They are utterly dependent upon typed cards which they receive from their press secretaries the moment they arrive in the office. These cards, broken down almost minute by minute, list every engagement of the day and every committee and subcommittee meeting, with a brief addendum of the agenda.
> They are dependent upon hasty briefings from aides who scurry alongside as they dash about the Capitol. Too often, their only time for studying a complex legislative problem is when they are driven to and from their offices by aides, wives, or chauffeurs.[53]

A legislative call system, consisting of electric lights and bells or buzzers located in various parts of the Capitol and House and Senate office buildings, alerts people to certain legislative occurrences. In the House, for example, the Speaker has ordered that the bells and lights comprising the system be utilized as follows: One long ring followed by a pause and then three rings and three lights on the left signifies the start or continuation of a notice or short quorum call in the Committee of the Whole that will be vacated if and when 100 members appear on the floor; two rings and two lights on the left note a fifteen-minute recorded vote, yea-and-nay vote, or automatic roll call vote by electronic device; two rings and two lights on the left followed by a pause and then two more rings notifies an automatic roll call vote or yea-and-nay vote taken by a call of the roll in the House; three rings and three lights on the left indicate a fifteen-minute quorum call in either the House or in the Committee of the Whole by electronic device; three rings followed by a pause and then three more rings represent a fifteen-minute quorum call by a call of the roll; four rings and four lights on the left, adjournment of the House; five rings and five lights on the left, any five-minute vote; six rings and six lights on the left, recess; and so on.

OUTLINE OF THE BOOK

The next seven chapters present case studies of congressional controversy. Chapter 1, by Jeffrey R. Biggs, former press secretary to then-Speaker Thomas Foley (D-Wash.), examines the battle over term limits that cost Foley his seat in the House of Representatives. Speaker Foley was caught in the cross fire between term-limit advocates at home in eastern Washington and his congressional colleagues on Capitol Hill. The discord surrounding this issue cuts to one of the essential conflicts of representation: whether legislators should govern as instructed delegates and respond directly to their constituents, or govern as trustees and use their own judgment to take positions they deem responsible, even when their constituents disagree with them. Foley chose responsibility over responsiveness on term limits, and this cost him his congressional seat. He followed the Burkean dictum that lawmakers should overcome parochial interests and accept a more independent role from their constituency, being free to act in pursuit of welfare and national interests.[54] Biggs provides an inside look at the internal tensions and external pressures that Foley faced when staking out his position on term limits.

In Chapter 2, Nicol C. Rae, a former American Political Science Association (APSA) congressional fellow who worked in the office of Senator Thad Cochran (R-Miss.) covers the race for Senate majority leader in the 104th Congress. Some of the most important votes in the House and Senate are those that select their party's congressional leaders. But electing leaders in the Senate is a far more daunting task than in the lower chamber, because Senate leadership, as a concept, remains more than a bit fuzzy.[55] If we are to believe floor leaders and scholars, the entire notion of "Senate leadership" is at least oxymoronic or, more likely, a simple contradiction of terms.[56] "Leading the Senate," reminisced former majority leader Howard Baker, "is like herding cats." So, by relative contrast with the impersonal, hierarchical and disciplined House, the Senate has continued to tolerate and even promote individualism,[57] reciprocity, and mutual accommodation.[58]

Chapter 3, by Paul S. Herrnson and Kelly D. Patterson, both former APSA congressional fellows who worked for Representative David E. Price (D-N.C.), explores the politics of agenda setting in Congress. Congress's agenda typically does not change incrementally.[59] Instead, major public policy changes happen all at once or in a flurry. Several different developments seem to come together at once to produce these changes. People on Capitol Hill identify and focus on certain problems rather than others, and they propose and refine policy proposals for reasons other than actually solving problems.[60] Of course, elections figure prominently into the agenda-setting process. In this chapter, two veterans of the agenda-setting process report on the intra-party conflicts that had to be overcome in order to craft, publicize, and disseminate the House Democrats' agenda.

In Chapter 4, David L. Leal, an APSA congressional fellow who worked for Senator John F. Kerrey (D-Mass.), examines the rancor and distrust over the 1999 congressional Juvenile Justice vote and how it exemplified an unorthodox approach to lawmaking on Capitol Hill. Changing patterns in congressional practice and procedure have worked to facilitate new styles of lawmaking; where the route to enactment used to be linear and predictable, now it is flexible and varied. Contemporary leadership is afforded more flexibility in shaping the legislative process to suit the specific legislation at hand, in advancing policy agendas, in challenging committee jurisdiction, and in accomplishing other goals. Leal reports on the growing use of unorthodox processes in lawmaking and assesses the subsequent affects on the committee system and the quality of the deliberative process. The Juvenile Justice vote of 1999 demonstrates how the contemporary lawmaking process provides congressional actors with more choices and how the alternatives they choose lead to different legislative paths. It highlights the range and variability of the contemporary legislative process. Congressional government may not be committee government, as Woodrow Wilson once held.[61]

Regardless of the emergence of new forums and procedures, each step of the legislative process remains a potential minefield for members of Congress seeking to enact legislation. Lawmakers can take a number of steps to increase the prospects of a legislative victory. These include building a strong coalition comprising congressional leaders and rank-and-file members; securing the support of the president, relevant interest groups, and the mass media; and rousing the public in support of the cause. As former

APSA congressional fellow Christopher J. Bailey illustrates in his discussion of the fate of tobacco settlement legislation in the Senate (in Chapter 5), failure to accomplish most, if not all, of these objectives can result in defeat, even when one of a bill's sponsors is a national hero, like Senator John McCain (R-Ariz.), and even when the group that would be most subjected to adverse effects of proposed legislation has low standing among the public, as does the tobacco industry.

Chapter 6, by Thomas L. Brunell, an APSA congressional fellow who worked in the House Subcommittee of the Census, uses original data to describe and analyze the battles that took place as Congress debated how to take the 2000 census. The decennial census, mandated in the constitution in order to reapportion seats in the House of Representatives among the states, has recently become one of the most partisan topics on Capitol Hill. In addition to determining how many House seats each state gets, the census is also used to redraw district lines within the states. The procedures that are used to count individuals have a major impact on the distribution and delineation of House seats. Also, the census is used to determine some federal budgetary allocations. Procedures that actually count heads often miss individuals, especially minorities, the poor, and residents of urban areas. This works to the disadvantage of traditionally Democratic states and the advantage of traditionally Republican states. Because they correct for undercounting, procedures that use statistical methods to correct for the deficiencies associated with enumeration work to benefit Democrats over Republicans. Attempts to switch from one method of head counting to the other is viewed by both parties as a war over which party will get to institutionalize an important advantage in the redistricting process. This chapter describes the battles that took place as Congress debated the methods to be used for the 2000 census.

Chapter 7, by Colton C. Campbell and Paul S. Herrnson, concludes with the lessons learned from the congressional battlefield.

Collectively, these essays show that Congress is a complex, cumbersome, and somewhat quirky institution. Its operations are governed by rules and norms and by the skills and personalities of those who apply them. Since Congress also moves at its own pace, meetings and votes are often moved up in the calendar, delayed, or put off indefinitely—and very rarely for reasons of scheduling alone. The number one reason that members of Congress bypass established rules, make more permanent changes in the way the institution operates, or reschedule a committee hearing, floor vote, or other exercise is to gain political advantage. Administrative efficiency, abstract theories of government, or the desire to find an algorithm that will perfectly represent the wishes of the American people are not high on the list of considerations that influence why members of Congress act as they do or how Congress operates. To paraphrase Senator Graham, government is not physics and Congress is not a supercomputer.

NOTES

1. Senator Bob Graham (D-Fla.), February 7, 2000, Miami, Florida.
2. Walter J. Stone, *Republic at Risk: Self-Interest in American Politics* (Pacific Grove, CA: Brooks/Cole Publishing Company, 1990), p. 14.
3. Roger H. Davidson and Walter J. Oleszek, *Congress and Its Members*, 7th ed. (Washington, D.C.: CQ Press, 2000).
4. Ibid.
5. John W. Kingdon, *Congressmen's Voting Decisions*, 3rd ed. (Ann Arbor, MI: University of Michigan Press, 1989); R. Douglas Arnold, *The Logic of Congressional Action* (New Haven, CT: Yale University Press, 1990); and David R. Mayhew, *Congress: The Electoral Connection* (New Haven, CT: Yale University Press, 1974).
6. Richard F. Fenno Jr., *Home Style: House Members in Their Districts* (Boston, MA: Little, Brown, 1978).
7. Davidson and Oleszek, *Congress and Its Members*, 7th ed., p. 420.
8. Richard L. Berke, "Lawmaker Takes Highway to Power," *New York Times*, 25 September 1997, A10.
9. Davidson and Oleszek, *Congress and Its Members*, 7th ed., p. 150.
10. Michael J. Malbin, *Unelected Representatives: Congressional Staff and the Future of Representative Government* (New York: Basic Books, 1980), p. 20. See also Thomas J. Klouda et al., *1996 House Staff Employment: Salary, Tenure, Demographics, and Benefits* (Washington, D.C.: Congressional Management Foundation, 1996), pp. 2–3.
11. Mark Murrary, "Top Aides Agree the House Is a Mess," *National Journal*, 27 June 1998: 1510–1511.
12. Norman C. Thomas and Karl A. Lamb, *Congress: Politics and Practice* (New York: Random House, 1964), p. 85.
13. Donna Casatta, "Swift Progress of 'Contract' Inspires Awe and Concern," *Congressional Quarterly Weekly Report*, 1 April 1995: 909–919.
14. *Congressional Record*, 106th Cong., 2nd sess., 22 March 2000: S1568.
15. Davidson and Oleszek, *Congress and Its Members*, 7th ed.
16. Ibid.
17. Ibid.
18. Ibid., p. 391.
19. Weingast and Marshall 1990; Kiewiet and McCubbins 1991; Gary W. Cox and Mathew D. McCubbins, *Legislative Leviathan: Party Government in the House* (Berkeley, CA: University of California Press, 1993).
20. Paul Light, *Artful Work: The Politics of Social Security Reform* (New York: Random House, 1985).
21. Barbara Sinclair, *Legislators, Leaders, and Lawmaking: The U.S. House of Representatives in the Postreform Era* (Baltimore, MD: Johns Hopkins University Press, 1995).
22. C. Lawrence Evans and Walter J. Oleszek, "Procedural Features of House Republican Rule," in *New Majority or Old Minority? The Impact of Republicans on Congress*, ed. Nicol C. Rae and Colton C. Campbell (Lanham, MD: Rowman & Littlefield, 1999).
23. Davidson and Oleszek, *Congress and Its Members*, p. 9.
24. Ibid.
25. Walter J. Oleszek, *Congressional Procedures and the Policy Process*, 3rd ed. (Washington, D.C.: CQ Press, 1989).
26. Ross K. Baker, *House and Senate*, 2nd ed. (New York: W. W. Norton & Company, 1995).
27. Joseph K. Unekis, "Committee Hearings," in *The Encyclopedia of the United States Congress*, vol. 2, ed. Donald C. Bacon, Roger H. Davidson, and Morton Keller (New York: Simon & Shuster, 1995).
28. Ibid.
29. Jeffrey Talbert, Bryan Jones, and Frank Baumgartner, "Nonlegislative Hearings and Policy Change in Congress," *American Journal of Political Science* 39 (1995): 391–392.
30. Harrison W. Fox Jr. and Susan W. Hammond, *Congressional Staffs* (New York: Free Press, 1977).
31. Daniel Rapoport, *Inside the House* (Chicago, IL: Follet Publishing Company, 1975), p. 18.

32. Benjamin Ginsberg and Martin Shefter, "The Presidency, Interest Groups, and Social Forces: Creating a Republican Coalition," in *The Presidency and the Political System*, 3rd ed., ed. Michael Nelson (Washington, D.C.: CQ Press, 1995).

33. James G. Gimpel, *Fulfilling the Contract: The First 100 Days* (Boston, MA: Allyn and Bacon, 1996); and Robin Kolodny, "The Contract with America in the 104th Congress," in *The State of the Parties*, ed. John C. Green and Daniel M. Shea (Lanham, MD: Rowman and Littlefield, 1996), pp. 314–327.

34. Benjamin Ginsberg, Walter R. Mebane, and Martin Shefter, "The Presidency and Interest Groups: Why Presidents Cannot Govern," in *The Presidency and the Political System*, 4th ed., ed. Michael Nelson (Washington, D.C.: CQ Press, 1995).

35. Colton C. Campbell and Roger H. Davidson, "Coalition Building in Congress: The Consequences of Partisan Change," in *The Interest Group Connection: Electioneering, Lobbying, and Policymaking in Washington*, ed. Paul S. Herrnson, Ronald G. Shaiko, and Clyde Wilcox (Chatham, NJ: Chatham House Publishers, 1998).

36. Stephen Engelberg, "100 Days of Dreams Come True for Lobbyists in Congress," *New York Times*, 14 April 1995, A12; and George Miller, "Authors of the Law," *New York Times*, 24 May 1995, A21.

37. Engelberg, "100 Days of Dreams Come True for Lobbyists in Congress," A12.

38. Jeff Shear, "The Ax Files," *National Journal*, 15 April 1995: 924–927.

39. James G. Gimpel, "Grassroots Organizations and Equilibrium Cycles in Group Mobilization and Access," in *The Interest Group Connection: Electioneering, Lobbying, and Policymaking in Washington*, ed. Paul S. Herrnson, Ronald G. Shaiko, and Clyde Wilcox (Chatham, NJ: Chatham House Publishers, 1998), p. 109.

40. Quoted in David Maraniss and Michael Weisskopf, *Tell Newt to Shut Up!* (New York: Touchstone, 1996), p. 111.

41. Ibid., p. 117.

42. Campbell and Davidson, "Coalition Building in Congress: The Consequences of Partisan Change."

43. Ibid., p. 88.

44. Joel D. Aberbach, *Keeping a Watchful Eye: The Politics of Congressional Oversight* (Washington, D.C.: Brookings Institution Press, 1990).

45. Roger H. Davidson, "Congressional Committees in the New Reform Era: From Combat to the Contract," in *Remaking Congress: Change and Stability in the 1990s*, ed. James A. Thurber and Roger H. Davidson (Washington, D.C.: CQ Press, 1995); and James A. Thurber, "Remaking Congress after the Electoral Earthquake of 1994," in *Remaking Congress: Change and Stability in the 1990s*, ed. James A. Thurber and Roger H. Davidson (Washington, D.C.: CQ Press, 1995).

46. Campbell and Davidson, "Coalition Building in Congress: The Consequences of Partisan Change."

47. Darrell M. West and Richard Francis, "Selling the Contract with America: Interest Groups and Public Policymaking" (paper presented at the annual meeting of the American Political Science Association, Chicago, 1995).

48. Gimpel, "Grassroots Organizations and Equilibrium Cycles in Group Mobilization and Access," p. 113.

49. Robin Gerber, "Building to Win, Building to Last: AFL-CIO COPE Takes on the Republican Congress," in *After the Revolution: PACs, Lobbies, and the Republican Congress*, ed. Robert Biersack, Paul S. Herrnson, and Clyde Wilcox (Needham Heights, MA: Allyn & Bacon, 1999).

50. Ibid.

51. Ibid., p. 79.

52. Quoted in Francis X. Clines, "Weary Political Noise, a Senator Sees a Peaceful Farm in Her Future" *New York Times*, 3 December 1995, p. 30.

53. Samuel Shaffer, *On and Off the Floor: Thirty Years as a Correspondent on Capitol Hill* (New York: Newsweek Books, 1980), p. 14.

54. Hanna Pitkin, *The Concept of Representation* (Berkeley, CA: University of California Press, 1967), p. 145.

55. Burdett A. Loomis, "Senate Leaders, Minority Voices: From Dirksen to Daschle," in *The Contentious Senate: Partisanship, Ideology, and the Myth of Cool Judgment*, ed. Colton C. Campbell and Nicol C. Rae (Lanham, MD: Rowman & Littlefield, 2001).

56. Ibid; and Roger H. Davidson, "Senate Leaders: Janitors for an Untidy Chamber?" in *Congress Reconsidered*, 3rd ed., ed. Lawrence C. Dodd and Bruce I. Oppenheimer (Washington, D.C.: CQ Press, 1985).

57. Randall B. Ripley, *Power in the Senate* (New York: St. Martin's Press, 1969); Christopher J. Bailey, *The Republican Party in the U.S. Senate, 1974–1984: Party Change and Institutional Development* (Manchester, GB: Manchester University Press, 1988); Barbara Sinclair, *The Transformation of the U.S. Senate* (Baltimore, MD: Johns Hopkins University Press, 1989); and Steven S. Smith, *Call to Order: Floor Politics in the House and Senate* (Washington, D.C.: Brookings Institution Press, 1989).

58. Ross K. Baker, *Friend and Foe in the U.S. Senate* (New York: Free Press, 1980).

59. John W. Kingdon, *Agendas, Alternatives, and Public Policies* (Boston, MA: Little Brown, 1984).

60. John W. Kingdon, "Agendas," in *The Encyclopedia of the United States Congress*, vol. 1, ed. Donald C. Bacon, Roger H. Davidson and Morton Keller (New York: Simon & Shuster, 1995), pp. 183–184.

61. Woodrow Wilson, *Congressional Government: A Study in American Politics* (New York: Meridian Books, [1885] 1956).

1

SPEAKER FOLEY AND THE FIGHT AGAINST TERM LIMITS

JEFFREY R. BIGGS

Some may regard it as heresy for a Democrat to admit, but the 1994 election was bound to happen some time. We had a very long run from 1954 to 1994, a forty-year period, which almost no parliament in the world has shared. And, one can argue, to some degree, the reality, or at least the threat of turnover, is a useful discipline on a parliamentary party. Otherwise, it's very hard to convince members that decisions have to be made, not only to accommodate differences, but that they involve real adjustments, real re-thinking, real restructuring, and not just depending upon the weaknesses of the opposition. The threat of the ax isn't necessarily sufficient. You have to actually feel the blade.[1]

So was the Foley narrative behind the defeat of the Democratic majority and the unseating of a House Speaker for the first time since the Civil War.[2] In 1964, the voters of eastern Washington's Fifth Congressional District unseated their twenty-two-year incumbent, Republican Representative Walter Horan, replacing him with a young, liberal, native son, Thomas S. Foley. Thirty years later that same district sent a message to the Capitol by defeating their representative at the acme of his influence as Speaker of the U.S. House of Representatives. Republican challenger George R. Nethercutt's campaign themes prominently featured a commitment not to "sue" his constituents and a pledge to abide by a three-term limit of service. This is the story of former Speaker Foley, that general of the defeated Democratic majority, and his ill-fated war against term limits.

CAUSE OF THE STRUGGLE: PROFESSIONAL POLITICS

The conjunction of three circumstances are required to defeat congressional incumbents: formidable opposition, firm reason to desert the incumbent, and enough money to acquaint voters with the challenger.[3] One veteran press correspondent in Washington state offered a localized variation: "Washington traditionally treats its incumbents kindly. Defeat of a sitting member of Congress is a rarity. But this year [1994], it's a political sin to be an insider and even worse to be a known Democrat."[4] Added to this was a political reality that had dogged Foley throughout his recent elections. "Republicans have spent years building a case against Foley and longing for the day they can recapture his conservative district," wrote the *Seattle Post-Intelligencer*. "They argue he has served too long. They say he can't serve three masters at once—his district, the Democratic Party, and President Clinton."[5]

After being approached by a number of local Republican Party activists about challenging the Speaker, George R. Nethercutt formally declared his candidacy for the Fifth District congressional seat in April 1994. Informally, he consulted Ed Rollins a year earlier. A friend of more than twenty years, Rollins's initial reaction was that "nobody beats a Speaker," but Nethercutt suggested that Foley seriously injured himself by supporting the lawsuit to overturn the term limits Washington state voters approved in 1993. The action "smacked of arrogance and proved Foley was out of touch with his constituents," he argued to Rollins.[6] Like the Greek Cincinnatus, Nethercutt would pledge to be a "citizen-lawmaker," promising to serve only three terms.[7]

Nethercutt's own February 1994 poll results suggested that Foley was vulnerable to a conservative challenger as long as that opponent was not a right-wing extremist, as Foley's last two challengers had been.[8] Nethercutt was this candidate. Intelligent, pleasant, thoughtful, he wasn't a screamer but a successful attorney who had been active in community affairs for years, headed the local Diabetes Foundation, and helped to start a nursery for abused children. He was the former chairman of the Spokane County Republican Party, a role that gave him an understanding of eastern Washington.[9]

Rollins, a one-time Robert Kennedy Democrat turned Reagan revolutionary, was one of the Republicans' quintessential hard-nosed professionals, having managed President Ronald Reagan's 1984 reelection campaign. He had headed the House Republican Congressional Campaign Committee, and temporarily served as co-chair of Ross Perot's 1992 presidential race. The Rollins method of political campaigning would bring something unfamiliar to the eastern Washington political experience: the emblematic political consultant. "Our strategy," he wrote when signing on with the campaign, "was to treat the Speaker with respect, thank him for his thirty years of splendid service, and give him his gold watch."[10]

In Washington state's all-party September primary, Nethercutt won 29 percent against two previous Foley opponents. "There ought to be term limits on

Foley. And there ought to be term limits on the number of times people can run against him," the first-time opponent quipped in an interview in Walla Walla, a university and wheat-growing town located in the southeastern portion of the state. Surprisingly, however, Foley captured just 35 percent of the vote during the primary, when just two years before, with constituent anger over congressional perks at its peak, he garnered more votes than all of the other candidates combined and more than twice as many as his nearest GOP rival.[11] In one poll released by Spokane's KHQ-TV shortly after the primary, Nethercutt emerged with a 58 to 39 percent lead over the Speaker, with three percent undecided. A spokesperson for Foley stated that the poll came "after six weeks of unrelenting attacks all focused on Foley . . . You don't emerge from that kind of battering unscathed."[12]

"For Thomas S. Foley," wrote the *New York Times* northwest regional correspondent Tim Egan, "who clearly loves Congress . . . this may be the most painful month of a distinguished political life. . . . Defending Congress gets him nowhere at a time when, national surveys find, only one person in five has any faith in it to do the right thing, and yet he must defend the legislative system that has made him its leader, or at least explain how his Speakership works to his constituents' benefit."[13] "There was some confusion about my being Speaker," Foley later noted. "There's no tradition for it. Nobody from the western United States had ever been Speaker before, and I think there was uncertainty about what the Speaker's job was and whether there was any benefit in having the local representative as Speaker. It was possible to argue that an inexperienced new member of Congress, devoting himself exclusively to issues of direct concern to the district, without the power, privileges, and position of the Speaker, would be a better representative. It was arguable with people that focus and intensity could make up for the influence of the Speakership."[14]

It was a debate that would not have occurred in the safe Democratic seats of former Speakers Thomas P. "Tip" O'Neill's Massachusetts or James C. "Jim" Wright's Texas, or even House Republican Leader Newt Gingrich's Georgia. Polls indicated, for example, that 60 percent of Gingrich's heavily Republican Georgia constituents did not object to his national role.[15] Both O'Neill and Wright were old-fashioned FDR Democrats who believed in federal spending at home and abroad, but especially at home. Constituents of Wright's north-central Texas Twelfth Congressional District, including Fort Worth and most of surrounding Tarrant County, had no doubt as to his value as Speaker. During fiscal year 1986, Wright delivered more than $5.5 billion in federal funds to Tarrant County; on a per capita basis, the figure topped all other congressional districts at $5,481.[16]

Foley, however, was more frugal in favoring his own district with federal largess. As a Democrat in eastern Washington, he long relied on crossover votes to win majorities in his Republican-leaning district. For at least a decade, Republicans trying to knock off Foley painted him as out of touch with his district, playing their perceptions of eastern Washington against "that 'other' Washington."[17] But every two years, like clockwork, Foley would dispatch them [his reelection opposition] with a series of debates or joint appearances, campaign swings through wheat country and timber towns, and rallies in Spokane.[18] Foley's campaign was so well-oiled a machine that observers argued his coattails helped Democratic presidential candidates Michael Dukakis and Bill Clinton win Washington in 1988 and 1992, not the other way around. But in the summer of 1994, the juggernaut was sputtering.

WHAT MADE 1994 DIFFERENT?

Since Foley's entry into the congressional Democratic leadership as House Majority Whip in 1981, he was forced to defend his role in crafting national Democratic issues to his Republican constituents. Two years of a Democratic Congress and presidency exacerbated the task, as did President Bill Clinton's rock-bottom popularity rating in the Fifth Congressional District, a challenge at which Foley and his staff were experienced. Beyond the attractiveness of the opposition, a major difference from 1992 and previous elections was that in 1994, national issues overwhelmed the conventional wisdom that incumbents retain their seats through well-tended constituent services and attention to local issues. Eastern Washington was second-guessing Tip O'Neill's oft-quoted wisdom that "all politics are local."

Foley's challenge to term limits and his support for both the Brady handgun bill and the assault weapons ban coalesced opposition to his reelection bid. In Ferry County, the Republican Party held a raffle. Before a large American flag was the prize available for a $1 chance: a Chinese-made, SKS semiautomatic assault rifle, equipped with folding bayonet.[19] In contrast to Nethercutt's opposition to the assault weapons ban, Foley, after a nearly thirty-year record of opposing gun control, came out publicly in support. The National Rifle Association (NRA), which previously supported him, launched an all-out assault on the Speaker, featuring actor Charlton Heston in ads opposing Foley.[20]

Foley suffered indignities that were unheard of in his campaigns of yesteryear. "For one thing, there are fewer and fewer people around who know that he is the son of Ralph and Helen Foley . . . who were so revered that their names are chiseled into the biggest new building at Gonzaga University, near the statue of Bing Crosby, who was a student there. Today talk radio hosts here call Mr. Foley things that are unprintable. Mr. Foley, in fact, seems perplexed at the degree of change he sees on the American political landscape." In an October byline column, *Spokesman Review* Managing Editor Chris Peck provided a flavor of Spokane talk shows. "It's not really about politics, as Todd Herman, the foulest mouth on Spokane talk radio, honestly said just the other day. 'When you are in talk radio you sit there and look at empty phone lines,' he said. 'I've gotta do what it takes to light up those phone lines.' Hence, the twenty-seven-year-old former Spokane Falls Community College student has tried to boost the ratings of KSBN AM 1230 by referring to Tom Foley as 'The Sphincter of the House.'"[21]

"If Tom Foley had set out to provoke a showdown with all the self-styled, populist movements of the decade," wrote The *Wall Street Journal's* David Rogers, "he couldn't have done a better job. From term-limit advocates and the National Rifle Association to radio talk show hosts and Ross Perot, the Speaker of the House is under a conservative assault. . . . Republican challenger George Nethercutt runs as 'Everyman' *vs.* that 'aristocratic' Washington on the other side of the nation."[22] However, if the Speaker proved vulnerable to the gun lobby because he had changed his mind, the same could not be said of term limits, which he had opposed from the beginning.

THE BATTLE OVER TERM LIMITS

Since the early 1990s, the growing national popularity of term limits had become an index of the increasingly partisan and hostile anti-Washington political atmosphere. Anti-Congress sentiment was institutionalized in a way unheard of a decade before, finding voice in a 1992 presidential candidate (Ross Perot), a radio personality (Rush Limbaugh), and a political agenda (term limits). In the process, critics of Congress transformed a largely silent mass of apathetic citizens into an organized force that turned up at lawmakers' town hall meetings, jammed telephone switchboards, and tended to vote in large numbers. Media treatment of Congress also took on an adversarial tone that many politicians and analysts suggested was palpably more strident than in the past. "There are more people now making it their stock in trade to deprecate their government," observed Senator Paul S. Sarbanes (D-Md.). "I will admit to some frustration when I find myself frequently put in the position of defending my character simply for being a member of Congress," said Representative Matthew F. McHugh (D-N.Y.) as he announced his retirement. "It's not healthy for the most fundamental institution in a democracy to lose the confidence of the country," Foley added.[23]

At a July 1989 National Press Club appearance by Speaker Foley, the subject of term limits was a mere sidelight in a discussion of campaign finance reform that was overshadowed by other issues, such as clean air, catastrophic health insurance, and the budget. "Some notion that there should be an artificial 50 percent decapitation of every incumbent in the legislative body every two or four years is a strange idea, in my judgment," Foley stated. "We in this country generally take the viewpoint that good performance should be rewarded."[24] A year and a half later, then–White House Chief of Staff John Sununu announced that President George Bush Sr. would support a constitutional amendment limiting terms for lawmakers.[25] Bush was seconded by

Vice President Dan Quayle who stated: "In the American spirit of change, let me offer an idea that will bring change. It is my contention that limiting terms of Congress will return choice to our elections and thus a positive and progressive change."[26] In charting his course, the president was following a well-beaten path of powerful Washington insiders running against the nation's capital in which they lived and worked. Opinion polls suggested that as many as 70 to 80 percent of the American public supported term limits regardless of political party, race, ethnicity, income, gender, or geographic location.[27]

During the fall of 1991, voters in the state of Washington were called upon to vote on Initiative 553. The measure proposed limiting the governor and lieutenant governor to two terms, state legislators to ten consecutive years (or three terms in the House and two in the Senate) and members of Congress to twelve consecutive years (two terms in the case of U.S. senators). Unlike other term-limit measures, Initiative 553 (I-553) was a "take-no-prisoners" approach since it would apply retroactively: If approved, all incumbents over the limit would be allowed to serve only one more term.[28]

Although the LIMIT (Legislative Mandating Incumbent Terms) movement began as a grassroots effort, the initiative, which needed at least 150,000 voter signatures to qualify for appearance on the Washington state ballot, received financial backing through a strange political alliance with out-of-state conservatives. The idea of term limits had clearly struck a public nerve. The petition that put I-553 on the ballot garnered the fourth largest number of signatures of any initiative in Washington's history. It was also unprecedented as the Citizens for Congressional Reform funds paid professional signature gatherers 40 cents per signature.[29]

One close follower of the initiative concluded that genuine populism had little to do with the drive: "This effort would never have made it on the ballot without the assistance of one out-of-state group. That is extraordinary for Washington State. This is an elite-centered campaign on both sides." On the other side were the League of Women Voters, most Washington state editorial writers, unions, the National Rifle Association, which was "very interested in seeing Tom Foley remain in office," and many of the state's largest employers, including Kaiser Aluminum and Boeing. "Every interest group in the state that has spoken has spoken against it. Every newspaper that has spoken has spoken against it," noted an observer, who then added, "It's going to pass handily." Populist or not, three months before the election some two-thirds of likely voters expressed support for the term-limits initiative, and seven weeks before the election, proponents enjoyed a 7.5 to 1 advantage in fund-raising.[30]

Inevitably, the Initiative 553 fight boiled down to a question of congressional clout. Older Washington residents remembered the glory days of "Maggie" and "Scoop"—the legendary "Gold Dust Twins," Democratic Senators Warren G. Magnuson and Henry M. Jackson—who insured a beneficial attitude by the federal government's hugely influential role in Washington state in such areas as the management of forest resources and cheap hydroelectric power symbolized by the U.S. Bonneville Power Administration. The major inheritor of that political legacy was Foley. In numerous staff meetings, Foley made clear his desire to avoid having the referendum seen as a vote on him. It was inevitable, however. By passing such a restriction, Washington would be the first state ever to cast away the power and prestige of the Speakership. Yet, as one analyst observed, "as Speaker, Foley represents more than anyone Congress's institutional identity. And it is the voters' resentment of the institution that is driving the term-limit movement."[51] It was also assumed that passage of I-553 would logically be challenged constitutionally by Foley, who would have the required judicial standing by being denied a place on the ballot.

Congress was slow to take term limits seriously. As the reform engine gathered steam, few senators or representatives wished to stand in the way of popular opinion. Representative Al Swift (D-Wash.), a highly respected and popular member of Washington's eleven-member delegation, understood his congressional colleague's reluctance in opposing term limits. Despite Foley's effort to dissuade him, Swift announced he would leave office in 1994 regardless of the I-553 outcome. "The frustration I have had, in speaking out against this very popular response [and] to the intense frustration people are feeling these days, is that, as a member of Congress, whose service to my district would be cut short by this initiative, I have no credibility."[32] An incumbent's opposition to term limits appeared to be little more than a crass, self-interested, effort to simply protect one's job.

As Speaker, Foley had no place to hide, and both he and his "clout" became known as "the Foley factor." As with previous opposition to constitutional issues of prayer in school, balanced budget, or flag-burning amendments, his challenge to term limits was rooted in the first Article of the Constitution. By restricting voters' choice, he felt term limits violated the Constitution's democratic principles. In the month before election day, Foley and then-Democratic Governor Booth Gardner were among those who asked the Washington state Supreme Court to keep I-553 off the ballot on constitutional grounds. "They're [supporters of the Initiative] wrong on this," Foley said. "I'm usually not categorical on this. But there is no, none, no legal case for the other side. It constitutes a legal fraud on the public."[33] The Washington state supreme court threw out the challenge, saying there was not enough time to consider the complex legal questions.

With no other options, Foley launched a media blitz against I-553. Nationally, on programs such as NBC's "Meet the Press" or KING, KOMO, or KXLY television in Washington state, it was a variation on a theme. "It's patently clearly unconstitutional applied to the Congress."[34] When term-limits proponents brought former California Governor Jerry Brown, a Democratic presidential nomination aspirant, to the state to bolster support, Foley reminded voters that as California governor he had proposed diverting Washington state water to his state. The effort was thwarted then, but term limits would reduce the state's defensive clout. "Finally," said Sherry Bockwinkel, Campaign Director of LIMIT, "we did the ultimate: We brought Jerry Brown to town. We were trying to show that this is not an exclusively conservative-backed idea, but little did I know that this is the stuff you find out afterward—that Jerry Brown was the governor that proposed taking our water. When you added together all these signs of California influence, it scared our voters right off."[35]

POST-ELECTION ANALYSIS

Defying conventional wisdom, voters rejected the Washington state term-limits measure by a 54 percent to 46 percent margin. Why the erosion of support in the Evergreen state and not in most other states? According to one analyst, "the Washington case was relatively rare in that well-known elites actively campaigned against the measure. . . . Foley was a well-known figure in Washington politics who symbolized the political establishment and whose tenure in Congress demonstrated the value of seniority."[36] "We had fully sixty-eight percent support up until the last few days," reflected Washington term limits coordinator Sherry Bockwinkel. "The number one reason was clout: 16 percent of the people said term limits would hurt us in Congress. These are the people who changed their minds in the last ten days prior to the election. . . . The Tom Foley blitz did not help us one bit. . . . Foley showed up and had total access to everyone in the media, unopposed views, and he just stormed around for four or five days and got blanket coverage."[37] The battle may have been lost, but not the war.

Bockwinkel indicated her intention to put term limits back on the ballot in 1992 with important changes, principally removing the retroactive provisions. It was assumed that by then more states would pass their own term-limits referenda, making Washington state seem more mainstream. Her key assumption for 1992, however, was that "all of the elected officials will be so consumed with their own reelection that they may leave us alone."[38] The strategy was to outflank the more difficult and time-consuming amendment process at the federal level and go directly to the voters and legislatures of each state. By mid-1995, voters or legislatures in twenty-three states, including the state of Washington, supported congressional term limits.

Another analyst suggests that the opposition message was not as important as the messenger. "Without Foley, the message would probably not have had the impact it did. . . . A year later in Washington, term limits supporters qualified another measure for the ballot. A coalition of interest groups, similar to the one in the previous year, opposed the measure. Foley, however, was preoccupied with his own 1992 reelection bid, and as a result was less active in fighting term limits."[39] The new term-limit restrictions were not retroactive and, to neutralize the loss of clout argument, would not go into effect until ten other states passed limits. This gave Washington state Democratic incumbents less incentive to oppose the measure. Most members also had their reelection hands full. In April 1992, soon after congressional "House bank" overdrafts became public, congressional approval plummeted, reaching an all-time low of 17 percent.[40]

Foley and other Washington state lawmakers who previously led the fight against term limits did not undertake the same effort in 1992. Each addressed it in the context of their own individual races. Foley had faith in the memory of the state's voters, who saw the flaws [in term limits] just a year previously. In November 1992, Washington state voters approved Initiative Measure 573 by a margin of 52 to 48 percent. Significantly, the measure failed, by a similar margin, in Representative Foley's own eastern Washington congressional district.

In a landslide victory, term-limits supporters prevailed in all fourteen states that held ballot initiatives limiting the service of House and Senate members, with Washington having the closest vote. Democratic consultant Vic Kamber, who fought to defeat term-limit initiatives in several states, laid the blame for his side's defeat at the feet of Democratic congressional leaders. Foley and others were lax in repairing the image of Congress, and were more interested in their own reelection campaigns than in taking on term limits. "If the leadership is not willing to defend Congress, then maybe these bozos deserve it," he said.[41]

THE COURT STEPS IN

At this point, however, the next field of battle over term limits would be fought in the courts. It was unlikely that a judicial term-limit challenge would go before the Supreme Court for at least two years because it would take over a year to work its way through the lower courts. Early in 1993 a series of meetings began in Washington, D.C., with Foley, Democratic members of the Washington congressional delegation, key staff, and representatives of a Seattle law firm that was hired to reinforce the League of Women Voters challenge to the Washington state term-limits referendum. The suit sought a declaratory judgment enjoining Ralph Munro and Christine Gregoire, the Washington secretary of state and attorney general, from enforcing the provisions of the referendum. One concern was that the challenge have "judicial standing" with at least one of the plaintiffs suffering injury to their rights if the term-limits provisions were to be enforced. It was assumed that, legally, standing would require a member of the Washington congressional delegation; politically, it would ideally be a member in a relatively safe seat. Representatives Jim McDermott from Seattle and Norm Dicks of Tacoma were considered "safer" than Foley in his always marginally Republican fifth district. Foley's staff argued that he was already vulnerable as point man on the

Clinton 1993 budget which, when passed, received no Republican vote and was labeled a Democratic "tax increase." Thus, signing on as a plaintiff against term limits might be one risk too many.

Foley was convinced that the 1969 Supreme Court ruling in *Powell v. Mc-Cormack* would prevail, was the senior member of the Washington congressional delegation, and was the Speaker of the House. For these reasons, it was his obligation to sign on as a congressional plaintiff against term limits.

One mitigating factor was that senior Republican Representative Henry J. Hyde of Illinois had filed an *amicus* brief supporting the challenge to term limits. Although disagreeing on a number of issues, Representative Hyde's brief agreed that the Constitution set forth exclusive qualifications (age, citizenship, and residency in the state) for service in Congress, and that, "as a Member of the House of Representatives" he also had an interest "in assuring that the effectiveness of the Speaker is not reduced by unconstitutional limits on his tenure."[42]

The plaintiffs' motions for summary judgment were granted by Judge Dwyer, whose ruling included a reference that "on June 12, 1787, the Constitutional Convention voted unanimously to reject congressional term limits. . . . In adopting a short but comprehensive list of qualifications for Congress—age, citizenship, and residency—the framers protected the "indisputable right [of the people] to return whom they thought proper to the legislature."[43]

One benchmark of the increasingly hostile anti-Washington, D.C. atmosphere of the 1994 election cycle was that, as of mid-February, twenty-one members of Congress had announced their retirements, a rate of projected departures exceeding previous levels. The virtual assurance of continued and significant congressional turnover might have tempered the ardor for congressional term limits, but U.S. Term Limits and other allies vowed to press on despite a federal court ruling against the 1992 Washington state ballot initiative. "A state may not diminish its voters' constitutional freedom of choice by making would-be candidates for Congress ineligible on the basis of incumbency," wrote Seattle's U.S. District Judge William L. Dwyer. Speaker Foley, now a plaintiff in the case, hailed the Dwyer ruling as a vindication of his own position.[44] But others saw it as a new political vulnerability for him in eastern Washington.

"I think some publication during my [1994] reelection campaign, maybe *Time* magazine, called the decision 'Foley's Folly.'" Foley recounted. He went on to say:

> I felt profoundly that this was an unconstitutional act. It was, by the way, never one in which I could be properly accused of standing in the way of my constituents because in both 1991, when it was defeated in the state, and 1992 when it passed, the majority of the Fifth Congressional District voted against it. You don't very often have a demonstration of where your constituents stand except to elect or not to elect you. In this case they voted for me, and against term limits.

Just as I voted on issues in the House when I thought members shouldn't be asked to do it if I didn't do it, I didn't think I could be an opponent of term limits and then be shy about joining the suit.

Well, if I'd known everything in advance, all the misunderstanding and confusion and so forth, I can't say I wouldn't have reconsidered, but at the time it didn't seem right for me to pass the duty onto somebody else. I was also the senior member of the [state] delegation. At the time, the law firm felt there was an issue of standing that could only be protected if there was a sitting member as a party to the suit. Now, as it happened, when the case went to argument, the standing issue was brushed aside. The presence of a member of Congress on the suit was totally unnecessary. In the meeting, the staff were concerned, and the lawyers' reaction was, "well, we understand if you can't do this, but it would be very helpful.

Throughout my career one of my own unspoken standards was that if I didn't take at least one vote a term that jeopardized my job, then I was maybe going down a slippery slide. If I went through a term never having felt that there was an issue of importance where my opinion was such that I hadn't taken an unpopular or dangerous vote then I ought to start a really serious debate with myself about whether I was becoming addicted to the office to the extent that I was compromising my views. The test was not my opinion. The test was the risk. In a conservative district there were generally a variety of risks and perils.[45]

That Foley's decision to join the suit made him politically vulnerable was subsequently borne out by his weak showing in the state's 1994 primary and, ultimately, the general election. Although his constituents had twice opposed a state referendum on term limits, in 1991 and 1992 Foley's legal challenge to the state-passed term-limits initiative drew charges in his opponent's ad that he was "suing his constituents" to get reelected.

Throughout a flagging campaign, Foley retained his ability to step back from the fray and coolly survey the damage:

You also have the sort of challenge the opponents of congressional incumbents pose to constituents of "you're not going to be bought" in your vote and opinion by the fact "Congressman Incumbent here has put in the street lights, or rehabilitated the court house, or provided funds for the local college, or paved the streets? You're not that kind of person are you?" And, with a variation on that argument: "Now that we have the benefits, shouldn't we question whether it wouldn't have been better if we hadn't had them at all? Would it have been more virtuous to have offered them up in support of smaller government or lower taxes? Now we can't tear up the streets or dismantle the courthouse, but one has to wonder whether this sort of thing is really good for the country. . . ." At times, one suspects, it's exciting to have the benefits of the projects and to reject the provider.[46]

IMPENDING DEFEAT

While many incumbents in both parties had misgivings about term limits, most members—other than Foley, Democratic Representative Al Swift of Washington state, and Republican Representative Hyde, who characterized term-limits backers as "a lot of sore losers at the ballot box"—were reluctant to take such a high-profile stand against a cause with such grassroots appeal.[47] More than 300 Republican House incumbents and challengers who signed the highly publicized Contract with America carefully pledged themselves to bring a term-limits constitutional amendment to the floor, even though they did not obligate themselves to vote for it.

"By knocking out powerful, long-serving Democrats, term limits are seen by many Republicans as the best chance to gain control of the House of Representatives, where Democrats have long been the majority party," reported the *New York Times* regional correspondent covering the Northwest.[48] In Washington state, term-limits advocates personalized their arguments, using Foley as their "poster boy." "It would be wrenching for him to give up the high salary, chauffeured limos, private accommodations paid for by the taxpayers, dinners with the President, Hollywood stars and return to the regular life of a taxpaying citizen in Spokane," wrote term limits advocate Sherry Bockwinkel in a statewide mailing.[49] The Bockwinkel caricatures and Rollins's campaign were almost synchronized, as one of the first Nethercutt television ads featured a long-standing tradition of providing the Speaker of the House with a car, in this case, a Lincoln Town car. "The Speaker has a limo the size of the president's," Rollins observed. "One of our first spots was about the Speaker and his big, black limo."[50]

Throughout their series of debates, Nethercutt repeatedly jabbed Foley for joining the League of Women Voters' lawsuit challenging the constitutionality of Washington term limits. "I pledge never to sue the people of this state, for any reason, under any circumstances," Nethercutt said at the first debate in Walla Walla. Foley's response was that his participation in the lawsuit had been misrepresented and that the courts must decide the constitutionality of the issue. He reminded Nethercutt that voters in the Fifth Congressional District rejected term limits, which the state narrowly approved in 1992. "All I did was hasten the opportunity to resolve the question," Foley said. "That's the first time I've ever heard someone say, 'I'm doing you a favor by suing you.'" Nethercutt fired back, stating he would support term limits, promising a self-imposed limit of six years on his service in Congress regardless of the lawsuit's outcome.[51]

Term limits was but one hotly contested issue in the campaign, but it was raised at every debate. "We have, in effect, a two-year term limit in the House under the Constitution. Every two years, every representative has to go before his constituents and make the case as to why he should be continued," Foley said in Spokane. Nethercutt called term limits sensible, seeing no problem with supporting them as law, even though the district's voters had bucked the state trend back in 1992. "I think if you asked those same voters today . . . I think they'd have a different view. That was the straw that broke the camel's back, the lawsuit."

A Speaker of the House in reelection difficulties made news, and eastern Washington was awash with local, regional, national, and even some international journalists covering the campaign. Foley could not be everywhere. If it was not Foley speaking to the issue, it was his staff. With so many "hot button" issues already on the table, why did the Speaker take this one on? Did he underestimate the risk? Foley's role in the term-limits debate, and subsequent lawsuit, hurt his popularity statewide. He knew it would, but he knew also that it was his role as Speaker—the only constitutionally mentioned officer of the House—to safeguard Congress from constitutional challenges.[52]

The term-limit issue also resonated in the daily Letters to the Editor column of the press. "One cannot and must not forget that Washingtonians voted in favor of term limits. Not only does Foley, our 'honorable representative,' take us to court over this issue, he demands the taxpayers pay his legal bill incurred in nullifying our vote!" wrote a Colville constituent. "It has become obvious whom Tom Foley represents in Congress and it isn't his constituency. When term limits were voted in, those limits were meant to apply to House Speaker Foley as well as the rest of the people we elect to represent us. . . . His motives are obviously self-serving and he can only be interested in maintaining his power base in Washington, D.C.," wrote a Spokane voter. "We do not need term limits. Our Constitution gives us voters the privilege of not voting for an elected official who doesn't perform to our satisfaction. Do not be misled by the voice of opposition. Tom Foley's records are in the *Congressional Quarterly*. . . . I urge you to read, and vote for Tom Foley," wrote another Spokane constituent.[53]

The issue proved to be more than rhetorical. Beginning in mid-October, "Crying Shame," a populist-sounding television advertisement, began airing in eastern Washington, which featured quotations from George Washington, Abraham Lincoln, and Harry Truman suggesting support for term limits. It closed with an appeal for people to urge Foley to support term limits. "Tom Foley . . . sued the people of Washington to prevent voter-approved term limits from applying to himself and members of Congress."[54] As reported in The *Wall Street Journal*, the ads were financed by a network drawing on wealthy Republicans with ties to libertarian and conservative causes and to GOP Rep. Newt Gingrich. Billing itself as a nonpartisan advocacy group, Americans for Limited Terms expected to spend some $300,000 to advance the term-limits agenda and not the defeat of any candidate, thereby avoiding Federal Election Commission rules requiring public disclosure and capping annual individual contributions. But Fred Wertheimer, president of the citizen lobby Common Cause, observed that "when a group is running TV ads in the closing days of a campaign that deal with a candidate for Congress, the presumption has to be that these are election activities, not issue advocacy."[55]

It appeared to be more than coincidence that the "Nethercutt for Congress" Spokane headquarters released an October 17, 1994, letter, on congressional letterhead stationery, from then-House Republican Whip Newt Gingrich alerting recipients that "this year we have the best opportunity ever to replace Tom Foley in Congress. Republicans in Spokane, Washington, have a winning candidate in George Nethercutt, Jr. . . . This campaign is a 'centerpiece' nationally for this year's elections. I hope you'll reach a little more and give the maximum financial support possible."

Even the Internet played a role in the fray, with Spokane's Richard Hartman, Treasurer for Reform Congress 94's "De-Foley-ate" project. Interviewed on a San Antonio, Texas, talk show, Hartman noted, "conservative talk show hosts all across America have been hearing people's dislike for Speaker Foley. When they hear of De-Foley-ate, they relate to it immediately and want to know more. . . . Foley's position on term limits was the most common topic. Callers expressed outrage at Foley's override of the term limits measure approved by Washington State voters. That may be the Achilles Heel that defeats Foley."[56]

Following a June 20, 1994 Supreme Court decision to review the legal status of state-imposed term limits, the issue finally came to a post-election head on May 22, 1995, when, in a 5–4 decision, the High Bench left a constitutional amendment as the only legitimate route for imposing such restrictions. As to Washington state and the other twenty-two states that imposed their own term limits, Justice John Paul Stevens, writing for the majority, noted that the framers of the 1787 Constitutional Convention considered term limits, but then deleted them. Specifically addressing an Arkansas-imposed term limits law in *U.S. Term Limits Inc. v. Thornton* and *Bryant v. Hill*, the majority ruled that the founding fathers wished to provide voters with a wide choice for their representatives in Congress and had fixed three specific qualifications in the Constitution—age, residency, and citizenship—and meant that list to be exclusive. "Allowing individual states to adopt their own qualifications for congressional service would be inconsistent with the Framers' vision of a uniform national legislature representing the people of the United States," wrote Justice Stevens.[57] This was essentially the argument Alexander Hamilton made in the *Federalist Papers*: "The qualifications of the persons who may . . . be chosen are defined and fixed in the Constitution, and are unalterable by the legislature."[58]

The May 1995 Supreme Court rejection of state-imposed federal term limits included a certain irony. The issue had been adopted by the 1994 Newt Gingrich–led House Republican Contract with America as a promise to bring a constitutional amendment to the floor, if not necessarily to vote for it. The Court decision had come on the heels of a U.S. House of Representatives defeat of that constitutional amendment to impose limits on members of Congress.[59]

In the last three weeks of the campaign, the Foley camp's own tracking surveys never reported the Speaker reaching 50 percent of the vote, while

President Clinton's popularity hovered at 27 percent. In early October, former Democratic Congressional Campaign Committee chairman and former House Majority Whip Tony Coelho (D-Calif.) criticized the failure of "the low-key congressional veteran" to go on the attack. "I have never attacked people in any of my campaigns, and I'm not going to do that in this campaign," Foley responded when asked by the press for a reaction.

Reporters who sensed an upset in the making questioned Foley's seemingly calm demeanor in the final weeks. By nature a very private person and not prone to much public revelatory reflection, the real answer to the question he kept to himself or, in part, to his closest congressional staff:

First of all, I had seriously thought about retiring in early 1994. I'd spent thirty years in the Congress and perhaps it was time to move on. But exit strategies are difficult when you're in the leadership. In the first place, you make the decision not just for yourself and your spouse, you make it for your staff and their spouses. . . . It's a heavy burden. The House gets consumed with leadership races when major vacancies occur. Even though the Speaker would inevitably have been Dick Gephardt in an orderly transition of continued Democratic control, the question of the majority leader might well have been contested . . . and the question of the Whip's job down through Caucus chair and vice chair would be open to other challengers. So you could have three races with all the candidates talking to all the members about hopes and ambitions in the midst of a final last-ditch effort to pass the administration's major undertakings. . . . George Mitchell had announced his intention to retire so we would have had leadership struggles going on in the House and the Senate, and I think by their very nature they're more disruptive in the House.

So, by the time I'd thought about it, and weighed all the alternatives and difficulties, it was very late in the game, and the election became one bridge too far.

Second, we were overwhelmed by a whole series of problems fighting off attacks by the term limits people, the National Rifle Association, and other groups such as anti-D.C. statehood. There was the unpopularity of the president in eastern Washington. Between 1994 and 1996 when he was reelected, the president's numbers doubled. The nadir was 1994. I've never, and don't, blame my loss on the President, but it was not a good climate for Democrats.

Third, the Speakership, which in other circumstances and geographies would be considered an impregnable advantage, was ironically a disadvantage in 1994 in eastern Washington. The approach of the opposition was: If there is any problem in the district, why hasn't it been corrected if the Speaker is so powerful? There was also the wonderful *argument* that you here in the 5th district are empowered more than any other people in the country. If you're sick and tired of what's going on in the federal government and Washington, D.C., you have a voice amplified beyond imagination in other parts of the country. They can only fire a member of Congress. You can fire the Speaker. It was a rather clever approach.

I think another factor in my alleged calmness was that we pretty much knew where we were all the time. We had very expensive but excellent polling. We reached the end of the race about a point behind. It was a question of whether it was going to come or not, and it didn't.[60]

OLD SOLDIERS NEVER DIE

An ironic footnote to Foley's reelection defeat came while he was serving in Tokyo as U.S. Ambassador to Japan. The *Seattle Post-Intelligencer* reporter Joel Connelly, who had covered Foley for so many years, wrote about a conservative Spokane talk show host whose relentless attacks on Tom Foley helped propel George Nethercutt into Congress. Richard Clear was now considering challenging the Republican incumbent in 2000 for the Fifth District congressional seat. "Clear," wrote Connelly, "is upset at Nethercutt's announcement that he will run for a fourth term in 2000 after pledging in his 1994 race against Foley, a Democrat, that he would serve only three terms and come home to Spokane." "The word I hear," as Clear was quoted, "is that even if George loses this race, he will stay back there. And these were the knocks against Tom Foley in '94, that he had become a Washington, D.C. beltway insider."[61] In June, Nethercutt made his announcement. As reported in The *Spokesman-Review*, "Sunday, he seemed to echo Foley's 1994 argument against term limits." "I have changed my mind," he was quoted at a Spokane press conference. "The work I started will not be finished by the end of this term. That is why I have decided to run again."[62]

Two hundred-plus years have passed since Edmund Burke spoke to the Electors of Bristol, England. "Your representative owes you," he said, "not his industry only, but his judgment; and he betrays instead of serving you if he sacrifices it to your opinion." A modern variation suggests that whether perceived or real, the vulnerability of American politicians has made it more difficult for them to make tough, independent decisions, court unpopularity, ask for sacrifices, fly in the face of conventional wisdom, or act in what their judgment tells them is in their constituents' or the nation's best interest rather than their own.[63] As Speaker of the House Foley subscribed to Burke's premium on legislative priorities such as civility, compromise, and bipartisanship. "I've taken positions that I think were damaging in a political sense, but I don't have any regrets taking them," Foley said. "I used to say that the most important thing about votes on the floor and positions you take in Congress is that when you consider them at election time you're able to say with some satisfaction that you can still vote for yourself."[64] But like Burke, Tom Foley's values came at the price of eventual defeat at the polls.

NOTES

1. Author's interview with Thomas S. Foley. I thank the Washington State University Press for allowing me to reprint portions of *Honor in the House: Speaker Tom Foley* (Pullman, WA: Washington State University Press, 1999).
2. The first Speaker to lose was William Pennington, a member of the Whig Party from New Jersey, in 1860. The second was his successor, Galusha A. Grow in 1862. See Stephen Gettinger, "The Defeated Speakers," *Congressional Quarterly Weekly Report*, 12 November 1994: 3291.
3. Gary C. Jacobson and Samuel Kernell, *Strategy and Choice in Congressional Elections*, 3rd ed. (New Haven, CT: Yale University Press, 1983); Paul S. Herrnson, *Congressional Elections: Campaigning at Home and in Washington*, 3rd ed. (Washington, D.C.: CQ Press, 2000), pp. 231–237.
4. David Ammons, Associated Press, "Incumbents Feel Heat," *Clark County Columbian*, 4 October 1994.
5. Joel Connelly, "Foley Displays Clout as He Prepares to Run for 16th House Term," *Seattle Post-Intelligencer*, 24 May 1994, A1.
6. Ed Rollins with Tom Defrank, *Bare Knuckles and Back Rooms: My Life in American Politics* (New York: Broadway Books, 1996), pp. 303–304.
7. Joel Connelly, "Nethercutt Keeps His Focus on Foley," *Seattle Post-Intelligencer*, 6 October 1994, A1.
8. Ed Rollins, *Bare Knuckles and Back Rooms*, p. 305.
9. Linda Killian, *The Freshmen: What Happened to the Republican Revolution?* (Boulder, Co: Westview Press, 1998), p. 19.
10. Ed Rollins, *Bare Knuckles and Back Rooms*, pp. 306, 324.
11. Jim Camden, *Spokesman-Review*, 22 September 1994, C1.
12. "Congress Daily Hill Briefs," *National Journal*, 23 September 1994, 3.
13. Timothy Egan, "The 1994 Campaign: The No. 1 Congressman and His No. 1 Test," *New York Times*, 29 October 1994, A7.
14. Author's interview with Thomas S. Foley.
15. Timothy Egan, "The 1994 Campaign: Foley Behind in Polls, Plays Gingrich Card," *New York Times*, 27 October 1994, A1, A26.
16. Bill Whalen, "Insight," *Washington Times*, 18 September 1989, 26–27.
17. Jim Camden, *Spokesman-Review*, 22 September 1994, A1; Christopher Hanson, *Seattle Post Intelligencer*, 15 September 1994, B1.
18. Jim Camden, *Spokesman-Review*, 22 September 1994, A1; Christopher Hanson, "Foley May Fear GOP Foe; Nethercutt Appeals to Crossover Voters, if He Wins Primary," *Seattle Post-Intelligencer*, 15 September 1994, B1.
19. Ibid.
20. Kenneth J. Cooper, "Toughest Test: Ross Perot Campaigns for Challenger in Final Push to Unseat House Speaker," *Washington Post*, 5 November 1994, A1, A9.
21. Timothy Egan, *New York Times*, 29 October 1994, A1, A9; and Chris Peel, *Spokesman Review*, 9 October 1994.
22. David Rogers, *Wall Street Journal*, 27 October 1994, A22.
23. Dave Kaplan, "Incumbents Call It Quits at Record Clip," *Congressional Quarterly Weekly Report*, 19 February 1994: 785–789.
24. Chris Harvey, "Foley Blasts GOP Plans to Boost Turnover on Hill," *Washington Times*, 25 July 1989, A3.
25. Charles Cook, "Political Surveyor," *Roll Call*, 13 December 1990, 12.
26. J. Jennings Moss, "Quayle Backs Move to Limit Hill Terms," *Washington Times*, 5 December 1990, A5.
27. Mark P. Petracca, "Rotation in Office: The History of an Idea," in *Limiting Legislative Terms*, ed. Gerald Benjamin and Michael J. Malbin (Washington, D.C.: *Congressional Quarterly Press*, 1992).
28. Dan Balz, "In Washington State, Politicians Face Showdown on Term Limits," *Washington Post*, 3 September 1991, A2–A3.
29. Janet R. Beales, "Washington State's Term-Limit Fever," *Wall Street Journal*, 20 September 1991, A12; and Timothy Egan, "Campaign on Term Limits Breeds Unusual Alliances," *New York Times*, 31 October 1991, A1.

30. Jeffrey A. Karp, "The Influence of Elite Endorsements in Initiative Campaigns," in *Citizens as Legislators: Direct Democracy in the United States*, ed. Shaun Bowler, Todd Donovan, and Caroline J. Tolberts (Columbus, OH: The Ohio State University Press, 1998), p. 155; and John Balzar, "Push for Term Limits May Rob Washington State of Its Clout," *Los Angeles Times*, 24 October 1991, A5.

31. Ronald D. Elving, "National Drive to Limit Terms Casts Shadow over Congress," *Congressional Quarterly Weekly Report*, 26 October 1991: 3105.

32. Susan B. Glasser, "Rep. Swift Won't Run Again in 1994: Cites Washington Term Limit Vote as Only Reason for Shocking Decision," *Roll Call*, 28 October 1991, A1.

33. Dan Balz, "In Washington State, Politicians Face Showdown on Term Limits," *Washington Post*, 3 September 1991, A2–A3.

34. J. Jennings Moss, "Washington State Comes to Terms," *Washington Times*, 28 October 1991, A1.

35. David M. Mason, ed., *Term Limits: Sweeping the States?* (Washington, D.C.: Proceedings of a Heritage Foundation U.S. Congress Assessment Project Conference, November 18, 1991), p. 29.

36. Karp, "The Influence of Elite Endorsements in Initiative Campaigns," pp. 157–159.

37. Mason, ed., *Term Limits: Sweeping the States?* p. 30.

38. Ibid., pp. 30–31.

39. Karp, "The Influence of Elite Endorsements in Initiative Campaigns," p. 163.

40. Jeffrey A. Karp, "Explaining Public Support for Legislative Term Limits," *Public Opinion Quarterly* 59 (Fall 1995): 374.

41. Thomas Galvin, "Limits Score a Perfect 14-for-14, but Court Challenges Loom," *Congressional Quarterly Weekly Report*, 7 November 1992: 3593.

42. *Brief of Amicus Curiae Henry J. Hyde in Support of Plaintiffs*, filed by Wilmer, Cutler & Pickering, before the U.S. District Court at Seattle, Washington, February 10, 1994, in the case of *Thorsted v. Gregoire*, 841 F. Supp. 1068, W.D. Wash. 1994.

43. *Thorsted v. Gregoire*, 841 F. Supp. 1068, W.D. Wash. 1944.

44. Ibid.

45. Author's interview with Thomas S. Foley.

46. Author's interview with Thomas S. Foley.

47. Holly Idelson, "Candidates Seeing Term Limits as a Top Vote-Getting Tactic," *Congressional Quarterly Weekly Report*, 15 October 1994: 2969–2971.

48. Timothy Egan, "Federal Judge Strikes Down Law Limiting the Term of Lawmakers," *New York Times*, 11 February 1994, A20.

49. Timothy Egan, "Lawyers Argue against Limits on Terms," *New York Times*, 12 January 1994, A10.

50. Rollins, *Bare Knuckles and Back Rooms*, p. 330.

51. John Wiley, Associated Press, "Nethercutt, Foley Outline Positions in First Debate,"*Daily Evergreen*, 19 October 1994, 1.

52. Staff Reports, "Face-Off for 5th District Debates: Nethercutt, Foley Clash over Issues," *Spokesman-Review*, 24 October 1994, A1.

53. *Spokesman-Review*, 8 September 1994; 12 September 1994; 11 October 1994.

54. Heidi Lutz, "Term-Limits Group Will Spend More to Defeat Foley," *Spokesman-Review*, 12 October 1994, B4.

55. David Rogers, "Conservatives Fund Campaign to Limit Terms," *Wall Street Journal*, 4 November 1994, A3.

56. *Spokesman-Review*, 15 September 1994.

57. Janet Hook, "Arkansas Case a Crucible in Term Limit Debate," *Congressional Quarterly Weekly Report*, 25 June 1995: 1679.

58. Holly Idelson, "Review to Be Turning Point for Term Limits Issue," *Congressional Quarterly Weekly Report*, 1 October 1994: 2802–2806.

59. Janet Hook, "Ruling Puts Term Limit Drive in Doubt," *Los Angeles Times*, 23 May 1995, A1.

60. Author's interview with Thomas S. Foley.

61. Joel Connelly, "Nethercutt: Decision by Clear Expected Soon," *Seattle Post-Intelligencer*, 4 August 1999, B1, B4.

62. Jim Camden, "Nethercutt Says He'll Run for Fourth Term," *Spokesman-Review*, 14 June 1999, A1.

63. Anthony King, "Running Scared," *Atlantic Monthly*, January 1997. King quotes fiscal conservative Democrat Representative Timothy J. Penny of Minnesota who retired in 1994 rather than run for reelection and, with journalist Major Garrett, wrote a 1995 book *Common Cents*. "Voters routinely punish lawmakers who try to do unpopular things, who challenge them to face unpleasant truths about the budget, crime, Social Security, or tax policy. . . ." Representative Penny could have included the issue of term limits.
64. Author's interview with Thomas S. Foley.

2

THE RACE FOR SENATE MAJORITY LEADER

NICOL C. RAE

The rise in the significance of political parties and party leaders has been one of the most significant developments in the Senate in the past half-century. In fact, the growing significance of leaders goes as far back as the 1920s, when the position of floor leader was separated from that of Caucus/conference chairman and formalized in the rules of both parties and in Senate precedents.[1] Until the 1950s, however, the position was usually held by less visible senators and appeared to be concerned primarily with "housekeeping" activities rather than with providing real leadership and direction for one or another of the parties in the Senate. Real leadership remained more informal and tended to be held by a handful of senators—William S. White's "inner club"—who enjoyed great authority due to the respect and awe in which they were held by their fellow senators, regardless of party.[2] Yet when the most distinguished Republican senator of the time, Robert Taft of Ohio, took the position of majority leader after the Republicans took control of Congress following the 1952 elections, it was an indication that the office might have more potential than previously realized. And in addition to the powers conferred on the floor leaders by their party Caucuses, Senate precedents gave the majority leader the right of first recognition in floor debate and, therefore, a powerful potential influence over the chamber's agenda if the leader chooses to exercise this prerogative.

In fact, Lyndon B. Johnson (majority leader 1955–1960) would largely define the modern Senate majority leadership. Johnson and his Republican counterpart Everett M. Dirksen of Illinois (minority leader 1959–1969) demonstrated how a majority leader could exercise control over the notoriously individualistic Senate and become a key political figure in Washington.[3] Subsequent Senate party leaders have not always followed the assertive

style of those two gentlemen and the power of the office has varied in the succeeding forty years. Nevertheless, it is apparent that the overall power and status of the party leadership positions has grown immeasurably since 1953.
Today's Senate majority and minority leaders are truly leaders of their parties
in the Senate and not mere servants of their fellow partisans.

Since the 1950s, the Senate party leader has also frequently functioned as
a *de facto* "leader of the opposition" or principal spokesman for parties not
controlling the White House. Johnson occupied this role during the 1950s,
as did Dirksen during the Kennedy and Johnson administrations, Howard
Baker (R-Tenn.) during the Carter administration, George Mitchell (D-Maine)
during the first Bush presidency, Robert J. Dole (R-Kan.) for the first two
years of the Clinton administration, and Trent Lott (R-Miss.) in Clinton's second term. Of course the extent of the Senate party leader's influence has varied according to whether the party in question controls the House of
Representatives and the political assertiveness of the party leader in the
House. When the Democrats lost the Senate but still controlled the House
during the first six years of the Reagan administration, House Speaker
Thomas P. "Tip" O'Neill (D-Mass.) was clearly the predominant party figure. When the Republicans finally gained control of the House in 1994, after
forty years, new House Speaker Newt Gingrich (R-Ga.) set the party's agenda for the 104th Congress (1995–1997) until his political eclipse following the
government shutdown of 1995–1996. Yet the general pattern has been that
when a party is either in a majority or a minority in *both* chambers in recent
decades, the Senate leader has been both more visible and more influential.
Aside from the personal factors involved, the general trend is surely attrib-
utable to a number of factors: the greater visibility of the Senate in the national
media consciousness; Senate involvement with issues of international policy and security matters that have featured prominently in American political debate since the onset of the Cold War, and that have survived the
conclusion of the latter due to America's unique global responsibilities; and
the Senate party leader's greater capacity, even when in a minority, to use
the chamber's lax debating rules to derail presidential initiatives.

All of this entails added importance in elections for the positions of majority and minority leader in the Senate, and in the leadership contest to be discussed in this chapter, the significance of being a national "party messenger"
would be a decisive factor in the eventual outcome.

THE MAJORITY LEADER RESIGNS

On May 14, 1996, while this author was working in the office of Republican
Senator Thad Cochran of Mississippi, a rumor was heard that Senator Dole
would resign as Senate majority leader, effective the following day. Dole had

already secured the GOP presidential nomination and it had become apparent that his position as both Senate leader and prospective nominee was having adverse effects on both roles. For weeks the Democratic minority had tied up the Senate to block passage of favored Republican measures—such as welfare reform—and pushed for their own favorite issues such as raising the minimum wage and the Kennedy-Kassebaum Health Care bill.[4] The Democratic filibuster was intended to expose GOP divisions, substantiate Democratic allegations that this was a "do-nothing" Republican Congress, and tie down the presumptive Republican presidential candidate and Senate majority leader with Senate business in Washington. It thus became apparent to Dole and other GOP senators that any bipartisan deal that would give both sides some of what they wanted would be impossible as long as the GOP presidential candidate held the Senate leadership, because the Clinton White House and the Democratic Senate minority did not wish Dole to get credit.

Dole decided to resolve the impasse himself with an unexpectedly bold move: On May 15 he announced his resignation, not only as Senate leader but also from his Senate seat, to concentrate on his presidential campaign.[5] Once Dole's resignation was announced it was regarded as inevitable in Senate corridors that Senator Cochran, chair of the Senate Republican Conference (the third ranking leadership position on the Republican side) would become a likely contender to succeed him.[6]

Cochran's office was a good perch from which to observe the race for Senate majority leader. Unlike the cramped offices in the House, Senate offices are like small corporations, with staff afforded substantial space and individual televisions, often tuned to the Senate floor, a party's policy committee's network, or to CNN. The atmosphere in this august body is calm, quiet, and professional in contrast with most House offices, which more closely resemble family businesses in terms of layout and formality. Senate aides are older and more seasoned than their House counterparts, many of whom are fresh from college. While most House aides see each other and their representative several times a day, socialize with each other, and call each other by their first names, the opposite holds true for the Senate. Senate aides stay largely behind their desks when not attending meetings and interactions. The constant striving for professionalism is a major characteristic of the Senate as an institution. In Senator Cochran's office there was no possibility of the kind of horseplay so prevalent on the House side. It can take an anonymous staffer weeks to work up the courage to introduce him or herself to a senator; to do so within just two weeks is by Senate standards positively aggressive.

On April 25, 1996, Senator Cochran announced that he would respect a six-year term limit on party officers passed by the Senate Republican Conference in the fall of 1995 and stand down as conference chair at the end of the 104th Congress (1995–1997). In view of subsequent events this decision seemed rather odd, but it was already expected that Senator Cochran would contend with his fellow Mississippi senator and party whip (number two in the Senate Republican hierarchy) Trent Lott for the position of majority leader at some stage in the not too distant future.[7] Office chat suggested that the decision to stand down (the new term limits deliberately exempted present incumbents in party offices) was partly a ploy to show that Senator Cochran was less "hungry for power" than his more ambitious Mississippi colleague. Whether the senator would have acted similarly had he known that the majority leader position would become open quite so soon is another question.

Senator Cochran's office swung into action immediately following the announcement of Dole's resignation. Since he had ousted the late John Chafee of Rhode Island as GOP conference chair in 1990, it was clear that Cochran had aspirations toward the Senate leadership. In that election Cochran had had the support of conservative senators against the moderate Chafee. Cochran's Mississippi Republican colleague and presumptive front-runner for Dole's job, Senator Trent Lott, was a very different kind of opponent, however. Elected to the Senate in 1988 (a decade after Cochran's first election) Lott had challenged and ousted Senator Alan Simpson of Wyoming (with the help of the votes of seven of the eleven conservative freshman Republican senators) as Senate GOP whip (or assistant leader) after the GOP regained the Senate majority following the 1994 elections. Senator Cochran perceived the potential threat of Lott's challenge to his own prospects of eventually succeeding to the leadership and he had tried to dissuade Lott from standing against Simpson:

> Alan Simpson and I had first been elected to the Senate in the same year (1978) and he was a close personal friend for whom I had a great deal of respect and affection. When Trent came to talk to me about running against Alan, I strongly urged him not to do it. He said that he really did want the job of Assistant Leader, because he had been an effective Whip in the House and Alan hadn't aroused enough enthusiasm for Republican initiatives in the Senate, and that as a party we weren't mean and aggressive enough, and as Whip, he could help us do better. I was impressed by his candor, but I was also alarmed because of my close relationship with Alan. Trent did not respond to my entreaties. He said he didn't want the leadership but he wanted to be Whip. I let him know that I could not support him for Whip. If he defeated Alan he would have a higher post than I had, and he would make it impossible for me to be Leader because the party would not want Mississippi senators to have the No. 1 and No. 2 positions. In that circumstance I wouldn't have a chance. We had a long conversation but we were on an obvious collision course. The next leadership race started the day that Trent defeated Alan by one vote. It put Trent in a position to win the next race and I was at a severe disadvantage.[8]

By ousting Simpson, Lott leaped ahead of his fellow Mississippian in the GOP Senate hierarchy and elevated himself to the position of front-runner should the majority leadership fall open. In fact, well before Dole's resignation, it was apparent that Lott held the "pole position" in any race to succeed him.[9]

Although both major leadership contenders came from the same state (an unprecedented situation in a Senate leadership contest), Lott and Cochran presented contrasting Senate styles and different versions of Republican conservatism.[10] Cochran was fifty-eight at the time of the election, Lott four years younger. Both men earned their B.A. and J.D. from "Ole Miss," and both were Baptists. Both were practicing attorneys and both had served several terms (six years for Cochran, sixteen years for Lott) in the U.S. House of Representatives. Cochran served in the Navy from 1959 to 1961 while Lott had no record of military service. According to Cochran, he and Lott have an amicable relationship, working closely on issues important to their home state. "Although we have been competitors," he said, "we have maintained a personal friendship and cooperative relationship in spite of that. We work well together to get benefits for the state and that is something that is often overlooked. There are cases in the Senate where senators from the same state and the same party don't get along and don't work together on legislation. We do work together and by and large we have a close working relationship and close personal friendship."[11]

Despite these surface similarities, however, there is little danger of confusing the two Mississippians. Senator Cochran is courteous, soft-spoken, and serious, resembling a traditional southern senator. Despite his Republican affiliation, one often feels that Cochran would have comfortably fit into the Senate of the 1950s and the old "inner club" of southern Democratic members, such as Richard Russell of Texas, J. William Fulbright of Arkansas, and (his former Mississippi colleague) John Stennis, so brilliantly characterized by William S. White in *Citadel*.[12] While highly articulate and widely respected for his seriousness and professionalism by his staff and fellow senators, Cochran has rarely sought the Washington limelight—instead being content to secure his political base in Mississippi, and working inconspicuously on the Agriculture and Appropriations Committees to serve Mississippi interests. Cochran is thoroughly conservative across the board—social issues, economics, and national security—reflecting the views of his state. But because of his thoughtful demeanor and low-key manner, he is not always regarded on Capitol Hill as a hard-edged conservative. Ironically, given his voting positions and his overthrow of the moderate Chafee for Conference Chair in 1990, Cochran was regarded as the more "moderate" contender in the race to succeed Dole.

Senator Lott, by contrast, was associated with the ideological conservatism pursued by the new Republican majority in the House of Representatives. While in the House, Lott rose as high as the number two Republican leadership position (whip) before moving to the Senate in 1988. As House Republican whip he worked with and encouraged Newt Gingrich and his associates in the Conservative Opportunity Society (COS) in their strident ideological assault on the Democratic Majority during the 1980s. Because of that association, Lott's one-vote victory over Alan Simpson at the start of the 104th Congress (1995–1997) appeared to reflect the new wave of conservatism sweeping the

GOP and Washington after the 1994 Republican landslide. All of this identified Lott as more "conservative" than his fellow Mississippian, but while his
manner was more voluble than that of Cochran, and he was a much more
eager and polished media performer, Lott was without the abrasiveness of
his old House ally, Speaker Gingrich. He comes across as a genial, backslap-
ping politician and shrewd political strategist inside the Senate, who is generally popular with his fellow Senators—even Democrats—and the news
media to whom he is highly accessible.[13] It is these media skills that would be
a decisive asset in Lott's leadership campaign. In congressional parlance, Lott
was more of a "showhorse" than the "workhorse" Cochran, and traditionally in a Senate leadership election that would probably have been seen as a
disadvantage. It is an indication of the extent to which the chamber has
changed since the 1950s, that the "showhorse" image actually helped Lott in
the race to succeed Dole.

THE CAMPAIGN

Senator Cochran spent most of the day of Dole's resignation on the telephone
to colleagues, trying to nail down commitments. But from the outset, the contest was an uphill struggle for Cochran. Cochran's biggest hurdle was the
widespread assumption within the media and in the Senate that the succession would automatically go to Dole's second-in-command, Lott. After all, a
majority of GOP senators had previously supported Lott's race for the whip
position only eighteen months earlier and Lott, himself, appeared to have
done the job well enough to feel confident of such continued support. The
largely conservative bloc of eleven freshman Republican senators (over half
of them former members of the combative Republican House minority under
Newt Gingrich) would also be a very difficult constituency for Cochran to
reach. "Trent had been a successful whip in the House," Cochran said, "and
there were a substantial number of Republican senators who had served with
him in the House." Cochran further stated, "They had personal bonds of respect with Senator Lott and they were an influential force in the Senate and
still are. Those senators formed the core of his support."[14]

Cochran faced an additional problem in the first few days after Dole's announcement; the highly respected and highly experienced Senate Budget
Committee chair—Republican Pete Domenici of New Mexico—also considered entering the race.[15] The Cochran camp was relieved when Domenici de-
clined to throw his hat in the ring, since the Budget chairman and the senior
Mississippi senator would have contended for the same bloc of moderate and
more experienced Republican senators.

The fact that Cochran came not only from the same region but from the
same state as Lott also meant that Cochran could not exploit regional differences within the Senate GOP to his advantage. After GOP Policy Committee

chair, Don Nickles of Oklahoma, decided to run for whip, and Domenici resolved to stay out of the leadership race, Republican senators faced a contest between two conservative Republican Mississippi senators with nearly identical voting records. In 1995, for example, both Mississippi lawmakers had a rating of 0 out of 100 from the liberal Americans for Democratic Action, while Lott had a 96 percent rating from the American Conservative Union (ACU) to Cochran's 83 percent.[16] The major difference between the two would be seen in style, not substance.

With the date of the election still dependent on the exact date of Dole's resignation, Lott, as usual, was fast out of the box, having anticipated that the leader's position would fall vacant at some point during 1996, whether Dole won the presidency or not. By May 17 Lott had garnered twenty-one public pledges of support with only twenty-seven required for victory. By contrast, Cochran's sole supporter was Indiana Senator Richard G. "Dick" Lugar.[17] Yet Cochran's forces still believed they could turn the election around. Senate leadership elections are notoriously unstable and public pledges had meant little in previous contests, especially where senators frequently pledged support to both candidates.

Cochran's staff was generally enthusiastic and upbeat about the senator's prospects. Although both Cochran and Lott were far too politically astute to make any public criticism of each other, there remained tensions between them that surfaced when Cochran staffers discussed the race privately among themselves. When Cochran announced his decision to run for an open Mississippi Senate seat in 1978, Lott apparently was irked that his House Republican colleague had not even consulted him on the matter.[18] Cochran's staffers, on the other hand, felt that Lott was something of an upstart, having leapfrogged ahead of their boss in the leadership hierarchy when his overall record was not comparable to Cochran's. Some of Cochran's more conservative aides also believed their boss was the more genuine conservative while Lott was the "slick" opportunist.

As the days passed, the original enthusiasm and optimism in the Cochran office ebbed as it became clear how successful Lott had been in creating a sense of inevitability around his candidacy. By May 16 they were clearly less buoyant, although the most senior member of the staff came up with a head count that gave Cochran a realistic chance of success if he could secure the votes of senior senators, committee chairs, and moderates. There was also the possibility that the Lott camp would become overly confident, bruise fragile senatorial egos, and thereby provide Cochran with an opening.

While the press believed the outcome was a foregone conclusion, Cochran took his campaign very seriously: "It's a personal thing in a Senate leadership election. I met or talked on the phone with every Republican senator and said that I would like to have their vote. But most of them had already made commitments to Senator Lott, and some friends suggested that I drop out."[19]

Cochran also began to do the rounds of major television shows in an effort to highlight his candidacy, although he was not as polished or comfortable on that medium as Lott. Despite the continued optimism of the staff, however, public pledges of support for Lott continued to mount. By May 25 Lott had secured twenty-eight pledges, more than necessary to win, including pledges from leading moderates such as James Jeffords of Vermont, John Chafee of Rhode Island, and Olympia Snowe of Maine, that the Cochran camp were counting on.[20] It was Lott's geniality, his media skills, and his effective performance of his vote-counting role as party whip that apparently counted more with Senate moderates than his ideological profile.

In Cochran's office business went on as usual; orchestration of the leadership contest was confined to the senator and his closest aides. Although all the staff, including the interns, were highly motivated there was little sense of a campaign or War Room atmosphere. The order of the day was professionalism, business as usual, and not a cross word about Senator Lott outside the office, especially to curious journalists who might try to telephone a visiting, unsuspecting congressional fellow to eke out information. After Dole announced that June 11 would be his last day in the Senate, the leadership election was finally set for the next day.

As the day of the vote approached and it was clear that there was no movement in Cochran's direction, there was little discussion of the leadership election around the office. One staffer who had been with the senator since his days on the House side twenty years previously, said she failed to understand why the GOP senators would prefer Lott to her boss with his far more obvious "senatorial" qualities. "Why he never even served!" she exclaimed, in reference to Lott's lack of military service by comparison with Cochran's naval service.

The day before the election, the office was silent about the leadership election and the probability that the boss was certain to lose badly. Later on the Senate floor, Dole made a moving farewell address that was conspicuous by its nonpartisanship; the outgoing Republican leader managed to mention more Democratic senators from his years of service than Republicans.[21] Cochran had come under some pressure to withdraw from a hopeless race, but he decided to stay in the contest up to the bitter end and force a vote of the Senate Republican conference, doing so out of loyalty to the few senators who made commitments to him.[22] Perhaps Cochran also felt that there was a point that had to be made to his staff and the voters of Mississippi, that he would not concede to his more junior colleague without a fight.

The final tally was announced the following morning. As expected, Lott won a resounding victory of forty-four votes to only eight for Cochran and one abstention. Cochran's very low total was probably artificially depressed by several of his backers jumping on the Lott bandwagon in the expectation that Cochran would withdraw before the vote.[23] At noon the staff gathered in the conference room of his office and the senator made a very generous speech, thanking the staff and telling everyone to work with the victorious Senator Lott. Cochran's dignified attitude toward a crushing defeat spoke volumes for his decency and character. In truth, he realized that he lost the election the day that Lott defeated Alan Simpson by one vote for the post of whip back in December of 1994:

> When I decided to run I thought that the campaign would be a more competitive race. As I said on the day of the election: I knew that I had a small base of support and during the campaign it got smaller! Trent Lott had gotten so many commitments. He started after he got elected as Assistant Leader. Quietly, but aggressively, he lined up a majority of the votes.[24]

After that, with Dole clearly focused on the presidential nomination, Lott never stopped campaigning to succeed him. By contrast, Cochran, out of deference to Senate norms, did not even start to campaign until after Dole announced his resignation on May 15.

WHAT EXPLAINS THE LOTT LANDSLIDE?

The Senate is supposed to be more tradition-bound than the House, more moderate, and more respectful of seniority.[25] How then could the more ideologically conservative Senator Lott, who had only been in the Senate for eight years, inflict such a crushing defeat on his Mississippi Republican colleague who had served more than twice as long and seemed to fit the mold of the archetypal Senate leader more closely?

The most important factor in Lott's victory was that the majority whip was better adapted to the American political environment of the 1990s on Capitol Hill and beyond. The principal battleground of contemporary American politics is television and Lott's telegenic qualities and verbal dexterity, which earned him unflattering jibes from Cochran aides, were better suited to this terrain than Cochran's superior qualities as a legislative craftsman. In fact, much contemporary politics in the Senate is concerned with "message," that is, articulating a partisan or ideological line to the wider viewing public external to the Senate chamber.[26] Lott learned message politics in the Gingrich House and witnessed its arrival in the Senate as well. Senator Cochran certainly believed that this was a factor in his heavy defeat:

> The House leaders seemed to want blood flowing in the streets and Trent Lott agreed with them. I didn't. I believed we should run the government in a way that reflected credit on the American people and in a civilized way. We needed some surety at the helm and a stable group of leaders that the people could trust. It was a matter of personality, temperament and decorum as much as policy. I agreed with them on a lot of issues.[27]

Thus it appeared that GOP senators supported Lott primarily because they saw him as the more effective party messenger, and message articulation is now a major part of a Senate party leader's job.

Reflecting external pressures from primary electorates, national party committees, and ideological PACs who provide much of the cash and personnel for contemporary Senate elections, the Senate has followed the House in a more partisan direction during the 1990s.[28] Partisanship and maintaining party unity have become more important in the Senate, and again the apparently more "ideological" conservative Lott seemed better adapted to this change than Cochran, who boasted of his ability to work with Democrats on the Agriculture and Appropriations committees. The class of 1994 was also active in introducing changes in the Senate Republican Conference Rules that suggested the possibility of Senate committee chairs being removed from their position for not toeing the party line; these changes had been prompted by Appropriations committee chair Mark Hatfield's refusal, in early 1995, to provide the critical sixty-seventh vote for the balanced budget amendment to the constitution. Senator Cochran certainly felt that these rules changes affected the leadership election:

> One of the reasons why the freshmen pushed the idea of having a legislative agenda and having committee chairmen approved by a secret ballot is that it gives the threat of retaliation some credibility. I recall the discussion in the conference, when it was said that members of the leadership refusing to go along with issues considered very important by members of the conference cannot be tolerated. . . .
>
> In the leadership race I saw so many chairmen line up to support Senator Lott. All the committee chairmen except two (who did not announce their vote publicly) voted for him over me. Even moderates like John Chafee and Jim Jeffords who is in line to be a committee chair. These changes have made the leadership more powerful by giving them a capacity to insist on party loyalty and discipline.[29]

But Lott also won the battle for Senate leadership because, while he could indeed play the role of rhetorical ideologue, he also came across to his fellow GOP senators as fundamentally pragmatic—a classic dealmaker in the tradition of Johnson, Dirksen, and Dole.[30] In fact Lott's willingness to accommodate and compromise was the main basis for the dislike of him felt by some of the more conservative members of Cochran's staff, one of whom privately referred to Lott as the senator from "Let's Make a Deal." Moderate members, such as Olympia J. Snowe of Maine, who had known Lott in the House, had always regarded him as someone who would do his utmost to accommodate their concerns. The shrewd, calculating, pragmatist side of Lott had already given him the unique distinction of having served as Republican whip (or chief vote-counter) in both the House and the Senate. In short, despite the media's eagerness to paint Lott as an ideological soulmate and ally of House Speaker Gingrich, the Mississippi senator had far fewer rough edges than the Speaker did.

So Lott won because he was the candidate who better reflected the Senate Republican Party and the Senate during the 1990s, and Cochran lost heavily in large part because of his adherence to traditional Senate norms and his distaste for the rise of partisanship and "message politics" in the chamber:

> Now there's a lot of posturing and a lot of speeches made but it's difficult to point to results. We have a stalemate and a lot of showmanship and confrontation on the floor urged on by the party leaders. We seem to be more concerned with making points for copy and headlines and not so much with making laws. It's become more like a debating society.[31]

While still apparently in the pragmatic tradition of Senate leaders, Lott had the telegenic skills to articulate the GOP message, and the ability to mobilize external partisan and ideological groups critical to ideological success.

Balancing these roles is extremely difficult, as Lott discovered in practice during his five years as majority leader from 1996 to 2001. In his first six months in office Lott played pragmatic deal maker as he made accommodations with the Democratic minority and the Clinton administration in order to pass vital compromise legislation—a minimum wage raise, welfare reform, immigration reform, the Defense of Marriage Act—that helped the Republicans retain control of the Congress in November 1996.[32] This pattern held through the onset of the 1997 budget deal and even after the onset of the Clinton administration scandals in 1998.[33] And although the Senate leader adopted a more partisan tone during the Monica Lewinsky affair, Lott also reached bipartisan agreements with the Democratic Senate minority on procedures for the Clinton impeachment trial that infuriated the House Republican "managers" who were prosecuting the president.[34] Yet, later in 1999, partisan imperatives led Lott to sabotage campaign finance reform legislation and the Nuclear Proliferation Treaty and, in May 2001, his attention to those imperatives at the expense of bipartisan consensus may have contributed to the sudden defection of Vermont Republican moderate Senator James M. Jeffords and the ensuing loss of the Republicans' Senate majority.[35]

Traditional Senate leaders saw their role as leading and catering to the interests of their fellow partisans inside the Senate and moving legislation when the opportunity for broad bipartisan consensus presented itself. These are still essential components of the party leader's role, but Senate leaders also have to play to a wider audience of ideological groups and activists affiliated to the party and more independent-minded members of the general public who cast the decisive votes in Senate elections.[36] For presidents of their party they are legislative managers and often virtual opposition leaders when the party does not hold the White House (after Gingrich's eclipse Lott came closer to playing this role). Senate leadership is now a job requiring multiple skills for different situations. And this requirement of political adeptness and versatility was decisive in Trent Lott's victory over Thad Cochran for the position of Senate majority leader in 1996.

NOTES

1   Robert L. Peabody, Leadership in Congress: Stability, Succession, and Change (Boston, MA: Little, Brown and Company, 1976); and Steven S. Smith, "Forces of Change in Senate Party Leadership and Organization," in Congress Reconsidered, 5th ed., ed. Lawrence C. Dodd and Bruce I. Oppenheimer (Washington, D.C.: CQ Press, 1993).
2. William S. White, Citadel: The Story of the U.S. Senate (New York: Harper & Brothers, 1955); and Donald R. Matthews, U.S. Senators and Their World (New York: Vintage Books, 1960).
3. Ralph K. Huitt, "Democratic Party Leadership in the Senate," American Political Science Review 55 (1961): 333–344; and John G. Stewart, "Two Strategies of Leadership: Johnson to Mansfield," in Congressional Behavior, ed. Nelson W. Polsby (New York: Random House, 1971).
4. Jackie Koszczuk and Jonathan Weisman, "Election Year Gridlock Grips the Capitol," Congressional Quarterly Weekly Report, 11 May 1996: 1275–1279.
5. Jackie Koszczuk, "Dole Leaves Senate behind to Hit Campaign Trail," Congressional Quarterly Weekly Report, 18 May 1996: 1357–1360.
6. Nicol C. Rae, Conservative Reformers: The Republican Freshmen and the Lessons of the 104th Congress (Armonk, NY: M. E. Sharpe, 1998).
7. David S. Cloud, "Lott Has Pole Position in 'Race' for Leader," Congressional Quarterly Weekly Report, 17 February 1996: 385–387.
8. Author's interview, June 5, 2000.
9. Cloud, "Lott Has Pole Position in 'Race' for Leader."
10. Jackie Koszczuk and Rebecca Carr, "From Ole Miss to Congress: The Lott-Cochran Rivalry," Congressional Quarterly Weekly Report, 25 May 1996: 1435–1439.
11. Author's interview, June 5, 2000.
12. White, Citadel: The Story of the U.S. Senate.
13. Cloud, "Lott Has Pole Position in 'Race' for Leader."
14. Author's interview, June 5, 2000.
15. Carroll J. Doherty and Steve Langdon, "Lott vs. Cochran: A Contest of Leadership Styles," Congressional Quarterly Weekly Report, 18 May 1996: 1361–1367.
16. Michael Barone and Grant Ujifusa, The Almanac of American Politics 1998 (Washington, D.C.: National Journal, 1997), pp. 905–906.
17. Doherty and Langdon, "Lott vs. Cochran: A Contest of Leadership Styles," p. 1309.
18. Koszczuk and Carr, "From Ole Miss to Congress: The Lott-Cochran Rivalry," p. 1435.
19. Author's interview, June 5, 2000.
20. Steve Langdon, "Lott Comfortably in Front in Senate Leader Race," Congressional Quarterly Weekly Report, 25 May 1996: 1440–1441.
21. Jackie Koszczuk, "A Farewell, Dole-Style," Congressional Quarterly Weekly Report, 15 June 1996: 1647.
22. Donna Cassata and Jackie Koszczuk, "Election-Year Politics Puts Added Pressure on Lott," Congressional Quarterly Weekly Report, 15 June 1996: 1643–1648.
23. Ibid.
24. Author's interview, June 5, 2000.
25. Ross K. Baker, House and Senate (New York: Norton, 1989).
26. C. Lawrence Evans and Walter J. Oleszek, "Message Politics and Senate Procedure," in The Contentious Senate: Partisanship, Ideology, and the Myth of Cool Judgment, ed. Colton C. Campbell and Nicol C. Rae (Lanham, MD: Rowman & Littlefield Publishers, 2001).
27. Author's interview, June 5, 2000.
28. Nicol C. Rae and Colton C. Campbell, "Party Politics and Ideology in the Contemporary Senate," in The Contentious Senate: Partisanship, Ideology, and the Myth of Cool Judgment, ed. Colton C. Campbell and Nicol C. Rae (Lanham, MD: Rowman & Littlefield Publishers, 2001);

and David W. Rohde, "Electoral Forces, Political Agenda, and Partisanship in the House and Senate," in *The Postreform Congress*, ed. Roger H. Davidson (New York: St Martin's Press, 1992).

29. Rae, *Conservative Reformers*, 157.
30. Langdon, "Lott Comfortably in Front in Senate Leader Race."
31. Author's interview, June 5, 2000.
32. Rae, *Conservative Reformers*, 182–190.
33. Carroll J. Doherty, "As Majority Leader, Trent Lott Discovers His Pragmatic Side," *Congressional Quarterly Weekly Report*, 11 April 1998: 931–935.
34. Carroll J. Doherty, "After Historic Swearing-in, Duty Trumps the Party Line," *Congressional Quarterly Weekly Report*, 9 January 1999: 40–44.
35. John Cochran, "For Now, Lott Stays as Leader," *Congressional Quarterly Weekly Report*, 26 May 2001: 1214–1215.
36. Burdett Loomis, "Senate Leaders, Minority Voices: From Dirksen to Daschle," in *The Contentious Senate: Partisanship, Ideology, and the Myth of Cool Judgment*, ed. Colton C. Campbell and Nicol C. Rae (Lanham, MD: Rowman & Littlefield Publishers, 2001).

3

CRAFTING A PARTISAN AGENDA IN THE HOUSE

PAUL S. HERRNSON AND KELLY D. PATTERSON

Following the 2000 elections, the Democrats found themselves without control of the White House or either chamber of Congress.[1] Facing significant rifts in both their House and Senate Caucuses, Democrats faced the daunting task of trying to craft a coherent message that would provide credible opposition to the Republicans. Although this was the first time in seventy years the Democrats had been without control of any major institution of the federal government, it was not the first time they found themselves divided over policy issues and needing to speak with a common voice. They were in a similar, but not identical, position when Republicans won control of both the presidency and the Senate in 1980. Reeling from the loss of these two institutions, Democrats sought to unify their party around a common legislative agenda and message in order to become a more effective opposition. They established a new agenda-setting process consisting of issues conferences, task forces, and a centralized communications operation. These new processes and structures lasted until 1992, when the Democrats retook control of the presidency and strengthened their majorities in the House and the Senate.

Congressional Democrats learned many lessons during their twelve years in exile from the White House. In this chapter we discuss some of the techniques House Democrats introduced for message and policy development in the late 1980s and early 1990s. As congressional aides assigned to the task of organizing the House Democratic Caucus's agenda-setting process, we had a rare opportunity to observe and participate in the challenges involved in setting policy directions in Congress. The process we participated in provides insights into the opportunities and pitfalls a congressional party confronts when it attempts to bridge the gap between legislative and campaign politics. It also provides general insights into the development and operation of the modern Congress.

THE SOURCES OF THE CHALLENGE

Even under the best of circumstances the House and Senate are difficult institutions to manage. Members of Congress represent diverse constituencies from around the nation. Members are ambitious and generally believe that they owe their election and subsequent reelection to their own efforts.[2] Furthermore, members have strong attachments to their districts and states. They believe that they should be free to pursue policies that their constituents elected them to pursue. They often view attempts by party leaders to set a policy agenda as intrusive. After all, what do party leaders know about what the people in Idaho or Georgia are thinking? For these reasons it is difficult to craft a message that transcends local interests. Furthermore, the party must compete with other congressional institutions for control. Committees jealously guard their jurisdiction and privileges. They see themselves as the primary vehicles for policymaking and may resist participating in or establishing procedures that potentially undermine their policymaking role.[3]

Developing a unified message is made even more daunting when the other party controls the White House. The leaders of the House and Senate must compete with the most heavily covered political institution in the nation and perhaps the world. The presidency possesses a vast public relations machinery that can create and respond to stories almost instantly. The executive branch is highly unified; virtually all of its political appointees owe their positions, at least indirectly, to the president, and their political fortunes rise and fall with his. Thus, the White House does not need to expend nearly as much energy as Congress on consensus building.[4] Moreover, the opposition party in Congress faces special challenges because legislators often strenuously disagree about whether it works to their advantage to support or oppose a popular president from the other party.[5]

The Democrats faced all of these challenges in 1980. The defeat of President Jimmy Carter by Ronald Reagan and the unexpected loss of the Senate left the Democratic Party reeling. Party members wondered openly about the reasons for such an electoral repudiation. Did the party lose because it was out of touch with the people? Did the party need to be more or less unified if it was going to recover? The debates raged among the faithful. This situation confronted Representative Gillis Long of Louisiana, chair of the Democratic Caucus. Long decided that the Caucus should take a more active role in framing a political message and policy agenda to compete with the Republicans. He established a set of task forces on policy topics and compiled the results into a booklet entitled *Rebuilding the Road to Opportunity*.[6] This effort was fairly unique in American political history in that it represented a congressional party's collective response to the positions of a governing presidential party. For reasons discussed earlier, members of Congress tend to resist such collective efforts.

Over time, however, the forces against such collective efforts proved to be fairly potent. The Caucus abandoned the task force process established by Long and cast about for other ways to oppose the Republican Party. At one level, the Democrats did not think they needed to maintain such collective efforts. Despite their standard-bearers' rejection at the polls in 1984 and 1988, Democrats were cementing their hold on the legislative branch. Since winning back control of the Senate in 1986, Democratic rolls had grown to 55 seats by the beginning of the 101st Congress in 1989. The numbers were even more remarkable in the House of Representatives. House Democrats had a remarkable 259–174 stranglehold over the Republicans. Many of these Democratic members of Congress were first attracted to public service during the activist 1960s, and had learned how to create and wield enormous power from the chairman's seat.

But as they chalked up yet another landslide presidential loss in 1988 (the fifth loss in six presidential elections), congressional Democrats were frustrated at their inability to capture the executive branch and fully realize their policy goals. Without the presidency, Democrats knew that many of their most important policy initiatives would be vetoed. Furthermore, the loss perpetuated the communications disadvantage the Congress would face compared to the White House. The Democrats recognized that they needed to change at least some aspects of their communications and policymaking processes.

THE MAJOR PLAYERS

As Democratic numbers grew in the House, changes in the Democratic leadership team brought to power a less ideological, more pragmatic set of leaders. Speaker Thomas S. Foley of Washington was determined to reduce the partisan atmosphere, especially in the wake of the bitter dispute over the ouster of former Speaker James C. "Jim" Wright of Texas. Foley often reminded partisans that he was "the Speaker of the whole House," not just the Democrats. He turned much of the party leadership responsibilities over to his deputies, primarily Majority Leader Richard Gephardt of Missouri—one of the original "Atari" Democrats first elected in the 1980s. Gephardt, along with the then-Caucus chair, Steny H. Hoyer of Maryland, and Caucus Vice Chair Victor H. "Vic" Fazio of California, saw an opportunity for House Democrats to lead an effort to develop new party policy positions that would help influence public perceptions of the Democratic Party and lay the groundwork for the 1990 congressional and 1992 presidential elections. This effort involved a communications group, referred to as the "Message Board," which was chaired by Fazio and run by Gephardt and his staff, and a set of issues task forces that were chaired by Hoyer. Representative David E. Price of North Carolina, a political scientist, state party activist, and advocate of strong parties agreed to coordinate the task forces at the member level through both the 101st and 102nd (1989–1990 and 1991–1992) Congresses. Representatives Dante Fascell of Florida, who chaired the task force on foreign relations, Robert E. Wise of West Virginia, who co-chaired the infrastructure task force with Robert A. Borski of Pennsylvania, and Robert T. Matsui of California, Marcia C. "Marcy" Kaptur and Louis Stokes, both of Ohio, and Ron Wyden of Oregon—the four co-chairs of the health care task force—were extremely active in the process. Hoyer, Fazio, Wise, and Charles Schumer of New York also were active participants in the message board.

Each of these members, and others, became involved in the Democrats' agenda-setting process for their own reasons, but a desire to help the party, promote specific policy concerns, protect their political turf, or advance their own political careers were among the most common motives. Fascell, who also chaired the House Foreign Relations Committee, was an expert on the subject and had deep reservations about President George H. W. Bush's approach to foreign policy. Fascell wanted to control the process to prevent the task forces from making recommendations that clashed with legislation produced by his committee. Wise was a young ambitious member, viewed by many as a rising star in West Virginia politics. He viewed chairing the infrastructure task force as a way to increase federal funding for rebuilding some of the crumbling roads and bridges in his state, while at the same time reducing unemployment. Kaptur, Matsui, Stokes, and Wyden—all strong advocates of improving the nation's health care system—were discouraged by the trends that had taken place under successive Republican administrations, including rising health care costs, inadequate insurance coverage, and cuts in Medicare, Medicaid, the Special Supplemental Food Program for Women, Infants, and Children, and other federal programs that serve at-risk parts of the population.

Career-related calculations were not far from the minds of some of these legislators. Price, Kaptur, Wyden, and Wise were relatively junior members who were looking to increase their recognition in the House or lay the groundwork for statewide races. Gephardt was laying the groundwork for a run for Speaker. Hoyer also wanted to move up the leadership ladder to the post of majority whip, which he won in the 108th Congress. Price, already admired by some colleagues for his studious approach to the legislative process, was interested in broadening his influence, mobilizing support for issues he thought important, and improving his committee assignments. One of his major goals was to win a coveted seat on the House Appropriations Committee.[7] These and other active participants viewed the task forces as vehicles for networking with colleagues, advancing their political careers inside or beyond the House, as well as influencing policy. Others viewed the task forces as forums to discuss issues normally debated in committees to which they were not assigned. Similarly, Hoyer, Wise, Schumer, and others who sought to raise their visibility viewed the message board as a vehicle for attracting the national spotlight.

Some 200 congressional aides had been assigned by their members to represent them in the task force process. Participation among staff, however, was just as uneven as participation among members. Most of those who were active in the process cared deeply about the issues. Many of the senior aides worked for members who were active in the process, staffing the message board or a task force as they would a committee or any other congressional activity. The more junior aides who became deeply invested typically worked for members who were somewhat less engaged. They considered the task forces forums for the policy influence they were denied elsewhere, as arenas in which they could sharpen their skills or prove their abilities, or as vehicles to expand their networks or move up to higher posts.

Our motives as American Political Science Association congressional fellows were somewhat unique. We wanted to observe and participate in the legislative process in order to make our own firsthand observations and judgments of some of the generalizations that routinely appear in the academic literature, as well as investigate new trends in party leadership and communications. We also wanted to hone and test our political skills. Working on this project for Representative Price gave each of us (Herrnson during the 101st Congress and Patterson during the 102nd) the opportunity to pursue our goals, with the blessings of an empathetic boss. Agreeing to coordinate a series of task forces and edit—and in some cases ghost write—the reports they were supposed to produce seemed to be ideal assignments for a couple of assistant professors who had strong interests in party politics and the legislative process. Our assignments gave us access to an extraordinary number of meetings of the Democratic leadership and to key players in the Democratic Caucus. We were among the few staff to attend the House Democrats' annual issues conference, and we were among the dozen or so persons in the room when Gephardt and other leaders would strategize about the party's message of the week and how to deliver it. Working closely with the Caucus staff, we were able to observe and participate in the challenges of trying to unify a party rife with faction. We also learned that coalition building involves more than simply getting members of different wings of the party to look for common ground on a specific issue. It also involves massaging big and sometimes fragile egos and catering to some of their professional and personal needs. We performed these chores to the best of our abilities, but inevitably we encountered some bumps in the process, some of which we discuss later.

OVERVIEW OF THE AGENDA-SETTING PROCESS

Each issues conference gave House Democrats an opportunity to develop a broad-ranging vision for the nation's future and to begin thinking of ways to communicate that vision to the public. Democrats understood that as the "out party" they needed to develop and publicize a political agenda to stand in contrast with the Republicans' agenda. Lacking such a vision, they would have difficulty giving voters a reason to elect one of their own presidential candidates. Democrats also understood that they would be at a significant disadvantage because a member of the GOP occupied the White House. The fact that the issues conferences always convened shortly after the president's State of the Union Address placed additional emphasis on the need to articulate and communicate the Democrats' philosophical and policy disagreements with the president. Indeed, Democrats had already tested some of these party themes immediately after the State of the Union Address. Various members of the Caucus would be selected to meet the press after the address and to provide the press with the Democratic "spin" on what the president had said.

The conferences also provided a sociological function. Party leaders intended them to provide an opportunity for House members to interact with each other. In the busy day-to-day flow of the House, members actually have little time to meet and get to know colleagues who serve on other committees or who come from different regions of the country. The leadership purposely set aside time for small informal group meetings where party leaders, committee chairs, and rank-and-file House members conversed and mulled over various policy proposals. Caucus staff monitored the groups and gauged the extent to which the groups seemed to be "getting along." Several former Caucus chairs, most notably Representatives Gephardt and William Gray of Pennsylvania, excelled at using the issues conferences and other agenda-setting activities to advance their standing with fellow House Democrats, the former becoming majority leader and the latter becoming majority whip.[8]

An ancillary benefit of the conference was the socialization of newly elected members to the House. The conference gave new members an opportunity to interact informally with the House leadership and to attend policy lectures and discussions with them. The smaller discussion groups also provided them with the opportunity to assess the issue positions of their colleagues. The format encouraged a frank and open discussion and gave junior members the courage to disagree with their senior colleagues. It is consistent with the "strategy of inclusion" that has been credited with helping House Democrats build consensuses on policy issues and function more smoothly as a congressional party.[9]

The conference was also designed to achieve a collective benefit. Leaders strongly hoped that the conference would promote cooperative behavior that would make the passage of Democratic legislation possible. To this end, leaders assembled the entire Caucus to discuss the various problems facing the party and the nation. They then divided the Caucus into working groups that consisted of ten to fifteen members to continue the discussion of major problems. Each working group was moderated by members of the Committee for Party Effectiveness, a group organized by the Caucus chairman to sponsor policy discussions, interpret polling results, and provide members with message expertise.[10] The moderators summarized and presented their group's assessments of the problems and recommended solutions when the entire Caucus reconvened. In this setting the Caucus devised a final list of issues that would serve as the agenda for the Caucus to pursue in the coming year. These determined the types of task forces to be created. Some issues consistently made it onto the Caucus's agenda, including the economy and health care. In 1982 task forces were formed to address seven policy areas: the economy, housing, national security, crime and drugs, small business, women's issues, and the environment. A few task forces were added or eliminated in later years to enable the Caucus to focus on current issues.

Each year the Committee for Party Effectiveness, with the approval of the Democratic Steering and Policy Committee, decided on the composition of the task forces for each of the issue areas identified by the Caucus. Each task force consisted of between fifteen and twenty members and had from one to four co-chairs to guide the work. At least one of the co-chairs normally chaired a committee or subcommittee with jurisdiction over that particular issue area. The chairs' involvement was meant to guarantee that the resources needed to draft a credible document were available to the task forces. It also helped reduce the friction between the task forces and committee chairs, many of whom were very protective of their authority and committee jurisdictions. The Caucus chair, vice chair, and task force coordinator all served as ex-officio members on each of the task forces. The staff from these offices provided the resources to manage the entire process and worked to ensure fidelity to the themes agreed to by the Caucus members at the issues conference. On average, 130 House Democrats participated in the task force efforts completed between 1982 and 1993.[11] Of course the involvement of members varied in intensity and supportiveness. Some members vigorously backed the process and others strongly opposed it, but most were somewhat neutral, participating only in aspects that interested them.

Party leaders also realized that it would not be enough simply to generate agreement on issues. The party would need to speak with a more unified voice and communicate its message to a wider audience. This realization led Gephardt to create the Democratic Message Board, a body designed to help House Democrats improve their overall presence on television and other media outlets.[12] Gephardt recognized that in order to overcome the cacophony of voices that seemed to emerge from the Caucus on a daily basis, the party's most visible spokespersons would need to meet regularly and coordinate their media outreach efforts. The Message Board was to be officially chaired by the Caucus vice chair, but Gephardt dominated its proceedings. The Message Board relied on the expertise of some of the House's more media savvy members. These members and their aides assembled weekly to agree on a message and to discuss the best way to present it, whether through coordinated floor statements, media advisories, or special events in Washington or around the country. The goal was to give these diverse communications a particular "spin" that favored the Democratic Party. The Message Board provided Gephardt with an opportunity to become a major party spokesperson and paved the way for him to become the House Democrats' leader and potential presidential candidate.

MAKING IT WORK

The late Speaker of the House, Thomas P. "Tip" O'Neill, Democrat of Massachusetts, is often quoted as having described his approach to the practice of politics with the phrase "all politics is local." Politics does not get more local than on Capitol Hill. With 535 members of Congress, five delegates, their staffs, the Congressional Research Service and a few other support agencies, Congress can be described as a small city. The House Democratic Caucus, however, is closer to a small town. Personalities and the political aspirations of elected officials and staff often become important factors in determining legislative action and policy outcomes. This was particularly the case with the task force process. There was resistance from various quarters throughout the process. Some members and staff simply resented the intrusion of the task forces into what has traditionally been considered committee work. Others were concerned that some task force members had ideologies and policy preferences that were out of synch with committee members and would lead them to make recommendations that clashed with bills reported out of committee. Still others did not participate out of apathy or because they were envious of colleagues who had been selected as task force chairs or co-chairs.

Some members and staff, including those who chose to participate, doubted the party's ability to unify around a message. Others feared that, should it succeed, any message that was disseminated would actually harm their individual chances for reelection. A number of conservatives, for example, were wary of task force reports that called for more spending—even when they agreed with the programs—because the documents would give their opponents the opportunity to attack them as "tax and spend liberals." Members sometimes reminded the Caucus staff that they, not the staff, would be facing reelection in the fall and the "wrong" national party message could harm their individual prospects.

All of these motivations and fears combined to create a process fraught with intrigue, personality clashes, and political hardball. Although the agenda-setting processes formally began at the House Democratic Caucus's Issues Conference held in January, two months of planning preceded the actual event. Staff worked to commission polls and focus groups to demonstrate to members the public's mood on major policy issues, the Democratic Party, and Congress. They also interviewed numerous professional facilitators to help figure out ways to bring members together into a meaningful dialogue on the party and its message. It was a struggle to get the Speaker to assent to the process and attend the conferences both in 1990 and 1992. He was generally wary of meetings that could later limit his ability to move the party in certain directions or result in the formation of rump groups for the disgruntled.

There were other distractions along the way. One year the Democratic Caucus held its retreat at the Greenbrier, a posh resort in the mountains of Virginia. The press decried the lavish surroundings and the presence of lobbyists. The next few retreats took place in more Spartan surroundings without the presence of interest group representatives or family members. The 1990 and 1992 issues conferences were held at the Marriott Hotel in Columbia, Maryland, and at the Mariner's Institute in Piney Point, also in Maryland. Both were open only to members and a limited number of staff. Because they featured none of the vacation-like trappings of other retreats, the executive director of the Caucus (in both Congresses) spent hours on the phone trying to convince members to attend them. The promise of good polling data and interesting conversation ultimately brought out most House Democrats. Some also came because they thought the retreats would be fun events, complete with fine wine and good cigars. They were not to be disappointed. In 1989 members even had the special treat of watching some of their colleagues perform in a spirited conga line. In 1992 members held a talent show complete with rock bands and cloggers.

Conference organizers anticipated that members would return from the retreat with a broader understanding of the challenges that faced their party and a shared sense of political purpose. Another goal was to build camaraderie among their diverse and sometimes factious membership. Finally, they hoped that members would leave the conference more willing to participate in the task forces, contribute to the crafting of a unified message that espoused the party's core values, campaign on that message as much as possible, and support the party's values in committees and on the House floor.

The Caucus chair, in consultation with members of the Committee on Party Effectiveness and other party leaders, appointed members to the various task forces. Some appointments were made prior to the issues conference; others were made in the weeks that followed. It was critical to get policy expertise on each task force so that it would have the resources to draft a sound document. Balancing regional and ideological concerns also had to be considered to make sure that no wing of the party felt its views had been left out. Seniority also was an issue, as committee chairmen and new lawmakers were purposefully assigned to the same task forces so the freshmen could learn how the House operates from their colleagues, and senior members could learn about the freshmen's concerns. With a proper combination of expertise and representation it was believed that the task forces could produce a useful set of reports.

Despite the best efforts of Caucus chair Hoyer and his staff, it was not always easy to secure the cooperation of individual members. In addition to the reasons discussed earlier, a few legislators held out for the usual quid pro quo, including one who withheld his assistance until he was assured that the Caucus chair would support increased appropriations for his committee's budget. Personal relationships also occasionally got in the way, as some task force members and staff avoided meetings when they believed someone they did not get along with might be present.

The Caucus organized nine task forces during the 101st Congress, one for each of the following policy areas: the economy, infrastructure, housing, education, health care, crime and drugs, environment and energy, foreign relations, and defense. Task forces on children, employment, and government waste were added and the task force on infrastructure was dissolved during the 102nd Congress. The performances of the individual task forces varied tremendously. Some task forces met enthusiastically and produced documents that helped foster a policy consensus among Democratic legislators and contributed to the political debate with the Republicans. Other task forces were dysfunctional from the start and required copious amounts of oversight from the staff who were charged with leading the process. In a few cases, the members and staff of an individual task force were so disinterested that members of the Caucus staff and Price's staff found it necessary to write the reports for them.

The Foreign Relations Task Force proved to be particularly successful during the 101st Congress. Representative Fascell chaired all of the task force meetings and used committee staff to do much of the heavy lifting needed to prepare its report. His approach consisted of polling task force members and their staffs for ideas and instructing a committee aide to write the first draft. Subsequent meetings were used to revise the document and a final draft was produced in two months. The document had a strong coherent message that members later reported using on the campaign trail.

The task force on government waste also produced a strong document in the 102nd Congress, entitled "The Challenge of Sound Management." Then-Representative Byron L. Dorgan of North Dakota chaired the task force and used his influence with committees to secure their expertise and support. The task force developed concrete recommendations that members could recite about specific ways that Congress might reduce government waste and spending when pressed by political opponents or the media. The document was released in a series of press conferences convened by individual members in their districts. Some members even held press conferences in landfills to dramatize the "waste." The booklet was also mailed out to Democratic officials in state and local government. A large number of members and officials reported using the booklet to inoculate themselves from charges of wasteful spending and to stake out positions on government management reform that they could use in the 1992 elections.

Not every task force operated smoothly or produced a valuable document. The range and nature of the problems members and staff encountered when trying to write their reports varied from task force to task force. The Defense Task Force was particularly difficult to manage during the 101st Congress. Most members and staff showed little interest in participating, leaving it to a few dedicated aides, primarily from the offices of junior members, to do the research and draft a document. Only after a near-final draft had been circulated did staff from the offices of some more senior legislators become involved, and their participation was decidedly negative. Aides to two top Democrats on the Defense Committee made a great show of informing task force staff that their handiwork was unacceptable and unrepresentative of the views of House Democrats. However, it soon became clear that they had sought to make mountains out of molehills. The conflict was ultimately resolved at a meeting in the committee chairman's opulent office, where the two aides detailed their specific objections to an aide assigned to coordinate the task forces. The objections amounted to little more than the wording of specific phrases, which were changed to register the chairman's imprint. Nevertheless, the experience taught a lesson to those who had invested themselves in producing the document. It was not the inadequacy of their work that had caused the objections, but the fact that they had produced a useful document without the participation of aides who had been long-term fixtures in Democratic congressional politics. As one task force staffer exclaimed, "We wrote a darn good chapter without them, and they were so mad about having to jump on the train as it was leaving the station that they felt the need to put us in our place and remind us who was in charge!"

Substantial and not-so-substantial differences in ideology or perspective were sometimes at the root of the difficulties. During the 102nd Congress a member of the energy task force held up the adoption of the report because he vehemently disagreed with a nuance in the wording of part of the document. The member claimed that he could not assent to the document because it was his duty to protect a particular industry in his district. After several days of bickering and negotiations, the impasse was finally resolved by simply switching the word "would" to "could."

Although both the defense and energy task forces ultimately drafted useful reports, the processes that produced them did little to advance some of the latent goals of the process. Task force members and staff did not develop a shared sense of political purpose or camaraderie, except for the small core that had been most heavily involved in drafting the documents. Indeed, bad feelings emerged among a few participants where previously there had been none. Just as some task forces capitalized on existing relationships and resulted in the formation of new ones, personality clashes among legislators and staff bedeviled the workings of others.

SUCCESSES AND FAILURES

The issues conferences and task forces subsisted in a culture that badly needed such mechanisms but remained generally suspicious of them. This must sound disconcerting to those who believe that the United States needs a more responsible party system. However, the processes did produce results that approximate some of the goals of responsible-party advocates.[13] For example, with an intense amount of commitment and effort, the Caucus succeeded in encouraging most members to frame many issues in the same way. In 1992 the Caucus helped dozens of members develop talking points and other information about health care reform. Most Democrats correctly believed that it would be a major issue in the 1992 elections and the party needed to stake its claim early to this issue. The Caucus also helped to organize and coordinate dozens of town hall meetings that members would hold in their districts on the same day. Party leaders hoped that the breadth of the coordination and commitment would demonstrate the party's seriousness about the issue. The ability of a party to demonstrate consistently to voters that it cares about a particular issue in ways different from the opposition is at the heart of accountability.[14] There also is some evidence to suggest that such activities produce another desired benefit—increased party unity. When political parties assist candidates with message development, the party unity among members of Congress increases.[15]

Second, the Message Board and the Committee on Party Effectiveness provided a more consistent avenue for getting out the party message. The Democratic Caucus even made some attempt at integrating these processes with the development of the 1992 party platform.[16] The organization of a mechanism to critique the party in power and to help members develop and discuss those issues makes it possible for voters to learn even more about the differences between the two parties and to make those differences a factor in selecting which party to support.

While these efforts help to reinforce the differences between the two parties, parties must also act on their promises. In other words, candidates from a party cannot say one thing and then turn around and govern differently. Realizing the importance of governing as a party, the Democrats made some movement to make party loyalty on some of these "core issues" an important consideration for elevation to committee chair or party leadership.[17]

Yet the experience of the task forces still fell short of the standards established by political scientists who favor responsible party government.[18] Much of the impetus for governing fell to President Clinton when he won the White House in 1992. Democratic leaders decided to support the president's agenda and suspended the task force process. Further, the products of the task forces really were not an "official party position nor a short-term legislative program but rather a set of goals and aspirations that Democrats seek to accomplish."[19] Not all members participated in the process, and there was no mechanism for punishing members who withheld their participation or opposed the process or its output. Members could and did participate or oppose the process in order to enhance their own careers.

LESSONS LEARNED

The history of the task force process reinforces much of the conventional wisdom about Congress. First, the strength of the electoral connection is a formidable obstacle to collective message development and policymaking. Representatives act to protect their own interests, which generally involve re-election and career enhancement.[20] Not many members are able to rise above their own interests to promote a party good. Indeed, the most effective way to solicit member involvement was for the Caucus staff to demonstrate to members how it could benefit their electoral efforts. This was particularly difficult to do when the member suspected that the task force process might infringe on a committee jurisdiction or upstage her own media efforts.

Members' interests, personalities, and egos often made it even more difficult to secure their cooperation. Some members saw themselves as the only expert on Capitol Hill in a particular policy area. They resisted any efforts to create other resources that might inform the public or other members. Other members withheld cooperation because they could not bring themselves to sit in a room with some other member, let alone cooperate with that person on the drafting of a task force document. The leadership needed to be aware of the jealousies and personality problems to complete the task force document.

The task force process also reveals the limits to which leaders will go to achieve a collective goal. The Speaker, majority leader, and whip approved the task force process, but they invested very little time and effort in it. These leaders left it to the Caucus Chair and his staff to assemble the coalitions and resources. The leaders' reluctance to invest their own political capital emboldened some members to resist and even undermine the process. In most situations there was very little that the Caucus staff could do in response. They were given much of the responsibility for carrying out a series of challenging tasks, but they did not speak from a position of authority and could not apply any sanctions. The staff relied on their members' support and on goodwill, which was often in short supply. Fortunately for the task force process, Hoyer held a seat on the Appropriations Committee during the 101st Congress, a privilege shared by Representative Price in the 102nd. Some members undoubtedly participated in the process so they would be in Representatives Hoyer's and Price's good graces when the Appropriations subcommittees considered member requests for special projects, although we saw no evidence that participants received any special treatment.

The Message Board and task force processes did demonstrate that the congressional parties can innovate. The issues conference and task force process provided a new forum that party leaders used to socialize junior members to the ways and norms of the House. Leaders recognized these benefits and consciously built them into the activities sponsored by the Caucus. The increased interaction between junior and senior colleagues may even have helped some junior members to enhance their communications and campaign skills. Bringing members together also may have led to some relationships that helped during elections, as the number of senior Democrats who helped their junior colleagues raise money increased during this period.[21] In this sense the party apparatus in Congress began to exert more influence in congressional and campaign politics. At the very least, the process helped to build a stronger sense of shared fate among House Democrats.

Furthermore, the Message Board and the Committee on Party Effectiveness reveal that the parties consciously think about message development and the best means for communicating with voters. In a political process increasingly defined by the mass media, the Committee brought in polling experts to provide members with information on the mood of the country and the best ways to talk about those issues. Members found these meetings helped them in exchanges with constituents as well as the local media. This shows the extent to which legislative politics has merged with campaign politics. It demonstrates that congressional parties help their members adapt to innovation.

Finally, the process reveals some of the reasons it is so difficult to achieve responsible party government in the United States. The primacy of reelection and the desire to preserve committee jurisdictions and other bailiwicks encourage members and staff to zealously guard their influence. They rarely cede power to institutions that seek to attain broader party goals. Moreover, bicameralism and the other checks and balances in the Constitution surely would have provided resistance to responsible party government had House Democrats been entirely successful in using the issues conferences, task forces, Committee on Party Effectiveness, and Message Board to get the Caucus to unify on the issues. Nevertheless, one of the major lessons learned is that when legislative party leaders commit themselves to a process designed to achieve some collective goals and they are able to convince members that their participation can bring them tangible benefits, it is possible for a legislative party to act in a more coordinated fashion.

NOTES

1. The Democrats temporarily won control of the Senate when Jim Jeffords of Vermont switched from being a Republican to an Independent but decided to caucus with the Democrats.
2. Paul S. Herrnson, *Congressional Elections: Campaigning at Home and in Washington* (Washington, D.C.: CQ Press, 2000), pp. 8–10, 252.
3. For a thorough discussion of these dynamics see David C. King, *Turf Wars: How Committees Claim Jurisdiction on Capitol Hill* (Chicago, IL: University of Chicago Press, 1997).
4. See George C. Edwards III, *The Public Presidency* (New York: St. Martin's, 1983).

5. For a discussion of the difficulties congressional parties face in a new media environment, see Paul S. Herrnson, Kelly D. Patterson, and John J. Pitney, Jr., "From Ward Heelers to Public Relations Experts: The Parties' Response to Mass Politics," in *Broken Contract? Changing Relationships between Americans and Their Government*, ed. Stephen C. Craig (Boulder, CO: Westview Press, 1996). For a discussion of the options a party faces, see William F. Connelly, Jr. and John J. Pitney, Jr., *Congress's Permanent Minority? Republicans in the U.S. House of Representatives* (Lanham, MD: Rowman and Littlefield, 1994).

6. Democratic Caucus, *Rebuilding the Road to Opportunity* (Washington, D.C.: Democratic Caucus, U.S. House of Representatives, 1982).

7. David E. Price, *The Congressional Experience*, 2nd ed. (Boulder, CO: Westview Press, 2000), p. 173.

8. See Ronald M. Peters, Jr., "Caucus and Conference: Party Organization in the U.S. House of Representatives" (paper presented at the annual meeting of the Midwest Political Science Association, Chicago, IL, April 2002).

9. Barbara Sinclair, "The Speaker's Task Force in the Post-Reform House of Representatives," *American Political Science Review* 75 (1981): 397–410; Barbara Sinclair, "House Majority Party Leadership under Divided Control," in *Congress Reconsidered*, 5th ed., ed. Lawrence C. Dodd and Bruce I. Oppenheimer (Washington, D.C.: CQ Press, 1993); and Barbara Sinclair, "The Congressional Party: Evolving Organizational, Agenda-Setting, and Policy Roles," in *The Parties Respond*, ed. L. Sandy Maisel (Boulder, CO: Westview Press, 1990).

10. On the Committee on Party Effectiveness, see David E. Price, *The Congressional Experience*, 2nd ed. (Boulder, CO: Westview Press, 2000), p. 172.

11. For a discussion of the regional and ideological distribution of participants in the task force process, see Paul S. Herrnson and Kelly D. Patterson, "Toward a More Programmatic Democratic Party? Agenda-Setting and Coalition-Building in the House of Representatives," *Polity* 27 (Summer 1995): 615–616.

12. For a brief description of some of the work done in this area, see George Stephanopoulos, *All Too Human: A Political Education* (Boston, MA: Little, Brown, 1999), pp. 21–24.

13. For a discussion of the assumptions of the responsible party model, see Chapter 5 in Kelly D. Patterson, *Political Parties and the Maintenance of Liberal Democracy* (New York: Columbia University Press, 1996).

14. See Constantine J. Spiliotes and Lynn Vavreck, "Campaign Advertising: Partisan Convergence or Divergence," *Journal of Politics* 64 (February 2002): 249–261. For an application of the same logic to presidential campaigns, see John R. Petrocik, "Issue Ownership in Presidential Elections, with a 1980 Case Study," *American Journal of Political Science* 40 (August 1996): 825–850.

15. David M. Cantor and Paul S. Herrnson, "Party Campaign Activity and Party Unity in the U.S. House of Representatives," *Legislative Studies Quarterly* 22 (1997): 393–415.

16. Price, *The Congressional Experience*, 2nd ed., p. 173.

17. David W. Rohde, *Parties and Leaders in the Postreform House* (Chicago, IL: University of Chicago Press, 1991), pp. 77–80.

18. See Committee on Political Parties, American Political Science Association, "Toward a More Responsible Two-Party System," *American Political Science Association*, supp. 44 (1950); and John C. Green and Paul S. Herrnson, *Responsible Partisanship? The Evolution of American Political Parties in the Post-War Era* (Lawrence, KS: University Press of Kansas, 2002).

19. Price, *The Congressional Experience*, 2nd ed., p. 173.

20. See especially David Mayhew, *Congress: The Electoral Connection* (New Haven, CT: Yale University Press, 1974).

21. Herrnson, *Congressional Elections*, p. 98.

4

UNORTHODOX LAWMAKING

JUVENILE CRIME LEGISLATION AFTER THE COLUMBINE SHOOTINGS

DAVID L. LEAL

Aside from impeachment, one of the most memorable events of the 106th Congress (1999–2001) was the series of votes on juvenile crime legislation. Not only were these among the most contentious in recent memory, but they also illustrate the changing nature of the legislative process in both the House and the Senate.

In the aftermath of the shootings at Columbine High School in Colorado, juvenile crime prevention suddenly became the highest priority on the congressional agenda. Coincidentally, two bills were making their way through the legislative process on a related subject, one in the Senate and one in the House. These would become the focus of legislative attention as Congress rushed to respond to the public outcry over school violence.

The Senate bill was numbered S. 254 and was officially entitled "The Violent and Repeat Juvenile Offender Accountability and Rehabilitation Act of 1999." The measure dealt primarily not with gun control but with reform of the juvenile justice system, and while somewhat controversial, S. 254 would prove a useful vehicle to which senators could add amendments. In the House, H.R. 1501 had bipartisan support and was relatively noncontroversial. As with S. 254, it would make a good vehicle for the many amendments members would want to make for policy and political purposes.

Congressional consideration of both bills not only illustrates the complex path of most high-profile legislation today, but it also contains some truly unusual legislative features. In the former category were several events that would have been rare decades ago but that are now increasingly common. For example, leadership in both chambers decided to bypass their judiciary committees and begin debate right on the floor, and in the Senate there was a filibuster by Democratic Senator Tom Harkin of Iowa.

There was also some unexpected drama, especially when the Senate reversed itself on an amendment to regulate sales at gun shows. It was initially defeated but after some legislative fumbling by the Republican leadership the Democrats were able to get a second vote. This time it reached the 50–50 mark on the morning of a school shooting in Atlanta, allowing Vice President Al Gore, the president of the Senate, to break a tie for only the fourth time in his vice presidential career.[1]

Accompanying the action in both chambers was a general tone of rancor and distrust that was only magnified by the memory of the recent impeachment trial. Democrats portrayed the Republicans as controlled by the National Rifle Association (NRA), while Republicans accused the Democrats of seeking not legislative solutions but a political issue to use in the next elections. Along the way, the original nature of the juvenile justice bills was largely overshadowed by the gun control amendments that became the central items of controversy.

THE CHANGING LEGISLATIVE PROCESS

The usual textbook discussion of how a bill becomes a law no longer provides a complete understanding of the standard operating procedure of Congress. It may be useful as a starting point in legislative studies, but as a description of reality it increasingly fails to ring true to those who watch it closely. Instead, a wide variety of formerly rare tactics and procedures are increasingly seen. Sinclair points out that while alternative paths have always been available to legislators, they are now used almost routinely, a phenomenon she calls "unorthodox lawmaking."[2] It is also becoming clear to other political observers. The *National Journal*, for example, titled a recent article on the legislative process, "How Congress Works: Not Always by the Book."[3]

The textbook description of House procedure begins with a member writing a bill and placing it in the "hopper," a mahogany box located near the Speaker's podium. The bill is then referred to the relevant committee for further consideration. If the committee approves the bill it is generally sent to the Rules Committee and then to the floor for a final vote. It may be amended in committee or during floor consideration. In the Senate, the process is similar but without the Rules Committee and with a reliance on unanimous consent agreements (UCA) or floor motions.

A decreasing number of bills follow this basic route today, especially those that are controversial. At every stage of the process, leaders and members now are more willing to use the institution's procedural options at their disposal. In the House, a bill may now begin its journey by being referred to several committees by the leadership instead of just to one, a legislative action called multiple referral. Some legislation will bypass the committee stage altogether, especially the politically sensitive and the time sensitive.[4] U.S.

president and political scientist Woodrow Wilson once held that the heart of the lawmaking process is the committee system, but this is increasingly untrue in recent decades.[5]

The House Rules Committee also assigns complex and restrictive rules—resolutions that structure the consideration of a bill from permissible amendments to length of debate—to an increasing number of bills, which limits the time allotted for floor debate and the number of amendments that can be offered.[6] Creative rules, such as *Queen-of-the-Hill*, allow members to be on all sides of an issue while allowing the leadership to still achieve their desired outcome.[7] There has also been an increase in postcommittee alteration of bills, including the relatively new "self-executing" rule that allows the leadership to make last-minute changes before a bill goes to the floor in order to increase the odds of passage.

This is not complication for its own sake, however, as procedures evolve over time and in ways that meet the needs of legislators. Which path the leadership chooses for a particular bill depends ultimately on its legislative goals. As Sinclair notes, "The new practices and procedures in the House facilitate lawmaking. Most make it easier for the majority party leadership to advance its members' legislative goals. The leadership now has more flexibility to shape the legislative process to suit the particular legislation at issue."[8]

Unorthodox lawmaking is also common in the Senate. The Senate has no functional equivalent to the Rules Committee and senators may talk for as long as they want unless sixty colleagues vote to invoke cloture and end debate. This leads to the possibility or threat of a filibuster, which used to be relatively rare but is now an everyday concern. This, then, increases the need for larger majorities and thus the necessity of compromise and postcommittee adjustments. There is no such tactic in the House, however, because representatives do not have the right to unlimited debate.

There is also no limit in the Senate to the number of amendments that may be offered nor to their content. In the House the Rules Committee can limit the number while the "germaneness" rule restricts amendments to topics relevant to the underlying bill. Senators increasingly take advantage of this opportunity to legislate. All these behaviors help make the overall lawmaking process more difficult because it requires extensive consultations and complicated UCAs to proceed. As Sinclair generally points out, "If the textbook legislative process can be likened to climbing a ladder, the contemporary process is more like climbing a big old tree with many branches. The route to enactment used to be linear and predictable; now it is flexible and varied."[9]

THE JUVENILE JUSTICE DEBATE BEGINS

The accelerated consideration of S. 254 began shortly after the April 21 shooting at Columbine High School that left fourteen students and one teacher dead. Although this was preceded by school shootings in cities such as Pearl,

Mississippi, Springfield, Oregon, Paducah, Kentucky, and Jonesboro, Arkansas, the one outside Denver was the deadliest in U.S. history. Even more shocking to the public was that it took place in a largely affluent area. While the public has long perceived urban schools as the most dangerous, neither Columbine nor the prior shootings took place in such a locale. Instead, the children of America appeared to be under siege in an unexpected and deadly way. As Senator Dianne Feinstein (D-Calif.) stated, "All of these took place not in Los Angeles, New York, Detroit, Chicago, Cleveland, or San Francisco, but in small suburban communities, many of them deeply religious, most of them middle to upper-class socio-economically."[10]

The preceding 104th Congress (1995–1997) had seen little legislative action on juvenile crime, and new gun control laws had not been passed since the assault weapons ban in 1994. The Senate Judiciary Committee did mark-up a juvenile crime bill in the first six months of the 105th Congress (1997–1999), but it never reached the floor because of opposition by both liberals and conservatives. Liberal members feared the provisions were too tough on young offenders, while conservatives worried it could be used to prosecute gun dealers and that the bill would become the vehicle for a gun safety-lock amendment.[11]

Democrats opposed S. 254 for a number of reasons. Although some changes were made as a result of relatively low-profile negotiations between congressional Republicans and Democrats and the Clinton administration, the feeling among Senate Democrats was that not enough progress was made.

First, the measure would allow federal prosecutors to try violent young defendants fourteen years and older as adults, while child advocates argued that only a judge should make that decision. Second, the requirement that juvenile offenders be separated from the adult prison population would be relaxed to allow "brief and incidental or accidental" contact and "accidental or incidental" communication. Child advocates opposed any such contact. Third, many Democrats argued that the bill spent too little on juvenile crime prevention and too much on prosecution.

The content of the legislation would not prove to be the main subject of debate, however. Instead, attention would focus on the large number of amendments senators would try to attach to it—"riders" that may or may not directly address criminal justice issues. Thus S. 254 was going to be the legislative vehicle onto which both Democrats and Republicans would offer provisions addressing not just juvenile crime but other issues such as gun control and violence on television.

Republicans were generally in an unsympathetic mood for additional gun control before Columbine. Then-Senate Majority Leader Trent Lott (R-Miss.) had earlier suggested that a good way to combat crime was not more gun control laws but increasing gun ownership: "Everyone is scared except the criminals. The way to change that is, give the criminals something to be afraid of. That something is a well-armed public."[12] His opinion would change, however, and at one point Lott would find himself urging his Republican colleagues to vote yes on a Republican gun control initiative.

ACTION IN THE SENATE

Although it is generally thought that the House acts before the Senate,[13] legislative action in response to Columbine was first considered in the Senate in the spring of 1999. The very first actions in the Senate took place on April 27, just seven days after the massacre, with senators passing 99 to 0 a resolution expressing condolences to the families of the victims. Senator Lott also signaled a willingness to consider some types of federal gun control measures, telling reporters, "There are some things we can do, hopefully, to keep guns out of the hands of kids."[14] He also announced that at least one gun control measure would come up for a vote on May 11. This provided opponents two weeks to prepare their case against new restrictions and convinced Democrats not to immediately begin attaching amendments to current legislation.

Lott had two choices on how to proceed. One was to bring up the Juvenile Justice bill, S. 254, and the other was to wait and take up a House crime bill that was slowly moving through that chamber. The decision was made to strike quickly and bring S. 254 directly to the floor, thus bypassing the committee and dispensing with any formal hearings.

Members from both sides of the aisle tried to rally public opinion around their solutions. The White House held a May 10 "youth summit" on children and violence that included gun manufacturers, entertainment executives, and religious leaders but deliberately excluded the NRA. White House staffers also met with Senate Democratic staffers to discuss legislative strategy. The House Judiciary Committee, fresh from its impeachment votes just a few months before, held hearings on the causes of youth violence on May 13 and Lott created a youth violence task force to meet May 8 through May 9 to develop alternatives to expected Democratic gun control amendments.

The first action on the Juvenile Justice bill was a series of Republican and Democratic amendments. Although there were a large number of potential amendments that senators wanted to offer, the leadership of both parties worked hard to whittle them down to a manageable number.

One of the realities of the contemporary Congress is the increasing number of members who want to offer amendments. While this tendency can be checked in the House through rules that restrict the number of such amendments, there is no such mechanism in the Senate. Instead, the leadership of the two parties must agree on the process, including the number of amendments and the length of time allocated for their debate. Even after several votes from May 12 through May 14, there were still seventy-five pending amendments and then-Senate Judiciary Chairman Orrin G. Hatch (R-Utah) threatened to kill the bill unless all votes were completed by the 18.[15] Democratic Senator Patrick Leahy of Vermont, ranking minority member of the Judiciary Committee, explained the difficulty:

> . . . as ranking member and floor manager on this side of the bill, I look at a whole lot of amendments. At one time, we had a couple hundred amendments.

> We whittled those down. Dozens of Senators on both sides of the aisle have agreed to withhold their amendments. I spent the weekend talking with senators, asking them to withhold their amendments. And they did.[16]

In the end, there were thirty-three votes or tabling motions on amendments covering a variety of gun and violence issues. Republicans offered sixteen such riders, Democrats fourteen, and three had sponsors from both parties.

The most controversial amendments were those on gun control. The first was a provision by Senator Frank R. Lautenberg (D-N.J.) to require background checks for all who wanted to buy firearms at guns shows, as the Brady Law did not apply to such purchasers. It was tabled 51–47, which is the functional equivalent of a rejection although technically only a refusal to take a formal vote. The Senate then voted to approve an alternative amendment by Senator Larry E. Craig (R-Idaho) that provided for voluntary checks at gun shows.

This unleashed a flurry of harsh rhetoric from Democrats. President Clinton said, "For the life of me I can't figure out how they did it, or why they passed up this chance to save lives. There is simply no excuse for letting criminals get arms at gun shows they can't get at gun stores."[17] "It shows we're all shocked by Littleton. But not shocked enough to stand up to powerful lobbies," added Senator Leahy, referring to the NRA.[18] U.S. Attorney General Janet Reno said, "I am stunned that less than one month after the worst school shooting in our nation's history, the Senate has decided to make it easier for felons, fugitives and other prohibited purchasers to buy guns."[19]

There were also second thoughts by some Republican senators. According to the *Washington Post*, "There was no great deluge of phone calls or lobbying against the original Craig amendment, congressional staff members said. Instead, the switch largely reflected a misunderstanding about what the measure actually would do. 'Some of the senators started looking at the language closely after Reno's complaint and some other things, and they realized that it wasn't as strong as they thought and that it needed to be fixed,' said a senior congressional aide."[20] Senator Gordon H. Smith (R-Ore.), for example, believed he was given the impression the gun checks in the Craig bill would not be entirely voluntary and "woke up angry at what we had done."[21]

In the face of such criticism and self-doubt, the Republican leadership scheduled a vote on a revised version of the Craig amendment, one that would make the background checks mandatory. It narrowly passed 48–47 on May 14, despite Democratic claims that it was "riddled with high-caliber loopholes."[22] Even so, the Republican leadership had to actively lobby its own members to ensure passage and avoid a very public embarrassment.

Democrats were not satisfied and on May 20 they brought up the Lautenberg amendment for a second vote, the fourth gun show vote in nine days. This time it passed 51–50 as Al Gore stood at the rostrum to break a tie. This was a stunning victory for Democrats and brought about much speculation about whether the power of the NRA was in decline. "What you just saw was the [National Rifle Association] losing its grip on the U.S. Senate at last," claimed then-Minority Leader Tom Daschle (D-S.D.).[23] It also gave the spotlight to the likely Democratic presidential nominee. "I, personally, would like to dedicate my tiebreaking vote to all the families that have suffered from gun violence," Gore said afterwards.[24] The Republican leadership considered denying Gore this publicity by encouraging at least one Republican to shift his or her vote from no to yes, but they apparently did not try this tactic.[25]

The Democrats got to fifty by gaining three votes—two from members who were not present at the first and one from former Senator Max Cleland (D-Ga.), who voted no the first time. His switch may have been a response to the shooting at Heritage High School in suburban Atlanta that wounded six students on the morning of the vote. The amendment also received six Republican votes, mostly from northern members. These included Peter Fitzgerald (Ill.), Richard G. "Dick" Lugar (Ind.), Mike DeWine (Ohio), George Voinovich (Ohio), the late John Chafee (R.I.), and John W. Warner (Va.). The sole Democrat to oppose the amendment was from Montana, Max Baucus.

This points out how senators may find constituent interests, personal beliefs, and partisan loyalties in conflict. One might imagine that the leadership of both parties would intensely lobby their members to vote the party line, but they must be careful in doing so. It does not help a party to win a vote by arm-twisting members to vote contrary to their constituents' views, as this could place them in electoral jeopardy. Party leaders understand that Democrats from more conservative regions and Republicans from more liberal areas may occasionally join with the other side out of both electoral necessity and personal conviction.

It is not often that a member of Congress receives a second legislative chance so soon after a defeat. One prominent example is from 1993, when former Senator Jesse Helms (R-N.C.) offered an amendment to grant a congressional design patent to a symbol of the United Daughters of the Confederacy, a symbol that included a Confederate flag. Former Senator Carol Moseley-Braun (D-Ill.), the first African-American woman to serve in the Senate, moved to table the amendment but her motion lost. She then vowed to filibuster "until this room freezes over" and gave an impassioned speech against the Confederate flag. The Senate then voted to reconsider its earlier decision and voted 75–25 to table the Helms amendment, with twenty-seven senators switching their vote.[26]

In addition, two controversial gun-related amendments failed to pass in the previous year but did so now. The first was a Feinstein amendment to ban "grandfathered" high-capacity clips for assault rifles. While federal law banned recently manufactured clips it exempted older ones. She failed in 1998 to attach this amendment to an appropriations bill, but on May 13 her very similar amendment passed on a voice vote after a tabling effort was defeated. Second, an amendment by Senator Herb Kohl (D-Wisc.), the owner of the NBA Milwaukee Bucks, to prevent the sale or transfer of handguns unless they had trigger locks passed on May 18. A similar amendment by Senator Barbara Boxer (D-Calif.) in 1998 was tabled.

The debate also saw a filibuster by Senator Harkin on an amendment by Senator Bill Frist (R-Tenn.), the only medical doctor in the Senate, to allow school officials to discipline special education students in the same way they do other students if guns or bombs are brought to school. While filibusters were rarely used in earlier decades, today they are increasingly used in parliamentary warfare and are especially likely for major legislation.[27]

It may also be difficult to tell the difference between lengthy but genuine deliberation and a desire to block a vote through filibustering.[28] As Sinclair notes, "when senators spend a long time debating and amending measure, they may simply be performing their deliberate function rather than trying to kill a measure."[29] In this case, what Harkin was doing only slowly emerged. After extended debate, former Senator John D. Ashcroft (R-Mo.)[30] asked for the yeas and nays on the Frist amendment. Senator Harkin did not yield the floor but said:

> Mr. President, we have had a pretty good debate, and it has been said that it has taken 2 hours. That doesn't bother me. I have spent years on this bill. I spent years on it. I spent my entire lifetime with a disabled brother. Do you think 2 hours means anything to me? It doesn't mean anything to me. We spent 3 years on this bill—3 years—bringing IDEA up to date. Do you think 2 hours bothers me? Not a bit.[31]

Senator Hatch, one of the debate managers, then went to the floor to see what was happening:

> Mr. Hatch: Will the Senator yield?
>
> Mr. Harkin: I am just getting started.
>
> Mr. Hatch: Will the Senator yield to his friend on the other side?
>
> Mr. Harkin: I yield without losing my right to the floor.[32]

After some discussion between Hatch, Leahy, and Harkin, Majority Leader Lott went to the floor to see if something could be worked out. Minority Leader Daschle then became involved and a UC was negotiated that set aside the pending Frist amendment, proceeded on several votes, and then returned to the Frist amendment with Harkin still holding the floor. This gave all parties time to work out an agreement while also getting some votes out of the way and allowing Harkin to keep the Frist amendment from an immediate vote.

Lott then threw in some humor, pretending to add the following to the UC: "Then I would add we would then pass this amendment [Frist] by voice vote. I was just kidding, Mr. President."[33] Harkin was not laughing and asked the presiding officer whether Lott's language was in the UC; Lott and Leahy assured him that it was not. Leahy also tried some humor during the filibuster: "Earlier this afternoon, I was speaking about crimes against senior citizens. If we stay on this much longer, the juveniles we are talking about today will be senior citizens that we may want to protect tomorrow."[34]

This is a good example of the "track" system, which allows Senate business to proceed even during a filibuster. Before it began in the early 1970s, all Senate activity was stopped when the right to unlimited debate was exercised. Now it is possible to have three or even four legislative tracks, assuming the majority and minority leader agree to do so or a UC is approved.[35]

Harkin relented the following day. As part of a UC it was agreed that his amendment on IDEA discipline would be accepted by voice vote after consideration of the Frist amendment. In addition, it may have been pointed out that many members of his party intended to support the Frist amendment, which meant that a cloture vote would eventually be sustained. Trent Lott announced the impending UC with some perhaps unintended directness: "I believe the procedure is that Senator Harkin would be entitled to the floor, but this unanimous consent agreement will take care of that problem and we will be able to move forward."[36] The Frist amendment passed 72–25.

The Internet also played a small role in the debate. An amendment by newly elected Senator Charles E. Schumer (D-N.Y.) to more tightly regulate Internet gun sales was tabled 50–43. Senators Hatch and Leahy jointly sponsored a less controversial amendment to encourage Internet service providers (ISPs) to make available free or cheap filtering software. It was approved unanimously, but it was largely a symbolic vote because most ISPs either already did so or were planning to do so.

Another subtext of the debate was whether the entertainment industry was to blame for Columbine and other school violence. Several of the amendments were therefore aimed at Hollywood. An amendment by Senator Mitch McConnell (R-Ky.) to require federal agencies to consider the violence level of a movie before giving permission to film on federal property was approved almost 2–1. An amendment by Senator Ernest F. "Fritz" Hollings (D-S.C.) to have the Federal Communications Commission (FCC) ban violent television during hours when children constitute a substantial portion of the audience was tabled by a wide margin, however.

Several of the amendments were considered in anything but a leisurely fashion. On several occasions the Republican leadership did not apparently notify Democrats about the exact topic of amendments. For those on the staff of a Democratic senator, it could be difficult to find out accurate information in the short time before voting began.

One source of information was a careful watch of the floor on the televisions located on every desk and in every room of the Russell, Dirkson, and Hart Senate office buildings. Both parties also sponsored their own internal television channels and information could sometimes be found on these. The Republican channel usually provided more information, but it was not always correct. On one occasion this channel gave a short summary of an amendment that turned out to be not quite accurate, but for some time this was the only information available to Democrats.

The leadership offices and committee staffers were a good source of intelligence. The "amendment desk," located on the Senate side of the Capitol building, was supposed to have a copy of all pending amendments, but this was not always the case. A last option involved going onto the floor and asking the staffers sitting on the benches along the back and side what was going on. The drawback was that it took valuable time to get there. One had to take the elevator or stairs to the basement, walk or ride the Senate subway through the underground passage to the Capitol, and then ride the elevators up to the floor staff entrance, check in, and walk onto the floor. In addition, sometimes the floor was full or the Democratic staffers had no better idea what the majority had in mind. While simply calling the office of the Republican senator who introduced the amendment might be considered an obvious solution, "crossing the river" was generally discouraged.

When floor votes were taking place, staffers with responsibility for the issue in question were usually found either on the phone, watching floor action on television, keeping senior office staff informed of current and anticipated events, and briefing and writing memos to the legislator. For staffers who handled gun control and criminal justice issues, days that may have passed calmly and without event when Congress was focused on other subjects suddenly passed with great speed and intensity. On several occasions the "day" did not end until late at night, when votes on amendments were taken one right after the other (or "stacked") after a full day of debate.

The last act before final passage of the bill and its associated amendments was a voice vote on the "managers' amendment," a collection of a large number of relatively noncontroversial items. Many were written by senators who did not have the chance to introduce amendments on the floor, thus enabling them to claim they made at least some small contribution aside from voting.

Some items allayed the concerns of many Democrats and child welfare advocates with the underlying bill, S. 254, which was almost forgotten during the debate. The language in the bill loosening the requirements to separate adult and juvenile prisoners, for example, was changed to reduce the odds of contact. Bill language would have changed the assumption that juvenile crimes should be tried in state courts, but this was adjusted to allow attorneys for juvenile defendants to challenge a federal prosecutor's decision to try the case.

The last word in the Senate debate was by Senator John F. Kerry (D-Mass.), who pointed out that S. 254 was not just about gun control and the criminal justice system but also contained funds for crime prevention:

> I am pleased we are passing a bill today which demonstrates we don't only begin to care about these kids . . . after the violence, after the arrest, after the damage has been done, when it may be too late—when we could have started intervening in our kids' lives early on, before it was too late. We can say that we have had a real debate about juvenile justice because we are passing a bill that makes some critical investments in vital early childhood development efforts, but a great deal of work remains undone.[37]

The final vote on S. 254, amendments and all, was 73–25, at which point all participants, from senators to their staff to lobbyists, were very tired. The wide vote margin came as no surprise, because as noted by Sinclair: "If legislation reaches the point of a passage vote, it almost certainly will pass. In recent Congresses the only major measures that lost on passage votes in the Senate were constitutional amendments, which require a two-thirds vote."[38] If a bill was too controversial to pass it would have died earlier in the process. As the next section will show, however, this does not necessarily apply to the House of Representatives.

In the aftermath of this "string of humiliating retreats and defeats by the Senate Republican leadership,"[39] there was criticism of Lott from both the left and the right. According to well-known Congress watchers Jack Germond and Jules Witcover, the votes represented a "woeful misreading of the public mood," and they criticized "the political and tactical misjudgments of Majority Leader Trent Lott."[40] Some conservatives also blamed him for the debacle, specifically for not pulling the bill when momentum shifted to the Democrats.[41] Lott responded that he had little choice: "Some people have been critical of me for, you know, allowing this debate to happen in the Senate. You don't *allow* debate to happen. It happens!"[42] In retrospect, there may have been little that gun control opponents could have done to avoid the issue, given the events at Columbine.

Lott was also criticized for allowing Senator Craig to serve as a high-profile point man for gun control amendments when he was also a board member of the NRA. This generated some bad publicity for the Republicans because it tied their legislative efforts closely to the controversial group, although aides claimed he was given the job because he knew the most about the substance.[43] As one observer generally noted, "On most of these issues Lott was damned if he did and damned if he didn't."[44]

Many Democrats hoped the momentum on this issue would continue in their favor. Said Senator Joseph R. Biden (D-Del.), "I just sense for the first time there's a real sea change."[45] This would be tested in the House debate.

ACTION IN THE "PEOPLE'S" HOUSE

After Senate passage, the action shifted to the House side. With Newt Gingrich no longer Speaker, this bill would be an important test of the leadership of newly elected Speaker Dennis J. Hastert (R-Ill.), who had been criticized for his efforts, or lack thereof, during House consideration of resolutions on the Kosovo conflict.[46]

The first decision of the Republican leadership was to delay the debate until after the Memorial Day recess, or about two weeks. Several things happened during this time. First, Speaker Hastert and Representative Henry J. Hyde (R-Ill.), then-chair of the House Judiciary Committee, began to develop a package of gun control provisions, including new checks on gun show purchasers and safety devices for handguns. They also signaled that parliamentary tactics would not be used to prevent consideration of gun control measures, as had been done in the past.[47]

Democrats as well as some Republicans criticized this effort, however. On the Republican side, former Majority Leader Richard K. "Dick" Armey (R-Texas) and Majority Whip Tom DeLay (R-Texas) let it be known that they would oppose such restrictions. President Clinton, speaking for many Democrats, said "It is a bill plainly ghostwritten by the NRA. . . . They've been calling the shots on this issue for decades now, and we have failed to do what is manifestly in the interest of our children and our communities."[48] Hyde responded the next day that, "The Democrats have one overarching goal—and it transcends gun control—and that is to see us fail."[49] Given that opposition was coming from the left and the right, including those who saw the legislation as either not tough enough or too tough, Hastert and Hyde had a difficult task.

The delay also allowed gun control opponents to work against the momentum generated by the Senate actions. The NRA in particular went on the public relations offensive. This included $200,000 for radio ads, $750,000 to send mail to all its members, $300,000 for phone banks to help generate calls to Congress opposing new gun restrictions, and full-page ads in major newspapers. It also lobbied representatives in districts where NRA members might be able to make a difference in the 2000 elections.[50]

The power of the NRA has long been feared in Washington because its membership is more likely to consist of active single-issue voters than is the group of people who support new restrictions. The Senate vote dimmed (temporarily, at least) the NRA's aura of invincibility and suggested the issue was becoming more salient to a growing number of people. In addition, the American Shooting Sports Council (ASSC), which represents gun manufacturers, had come to support some restrictions on guns and thereby partially broke with the NRA. Working against the NRA was the group Handgun Control Inc., the main lobby group favoring new restrictions, which promised to spend about $350,000 on advertising and grassroots activities in about fifty swing districts.

The House debate was therefore an important test of NRA power, and it needed a victory in the House to slow down the growing momentum for new gun control. The group argued that the answer to gun violence was not new gun restrictions but tougher enforcement of existing laws.[51] Many Republican lawmakers chided the Clinton administration for doing a bad job in this regard. "It is law enforcement that stops the criminal. . . . Janet Reno [attorney general], your record of law enforcement is dismal. You have winked and nodded at the law," charged Senator Craig.[52] Senator Hatch similarly noted that "We in the Senate must recognize that all the gun laws we could ever pass mean absolutely nothing if the Attorney General does not enforce them."[53]

When the recess was over and the time for consideration arrived, Hastert and the House Rules Committee, chaired by Representative David Dreier (R-Calif.), split the legislation into two parts: One bill would cover juvenile justice reform and the other would be the vehicle for gun control amendments.[54] The first was H.R. 1501, which as opposed to S. 254 was relatively noncontroversial and had been adopted by a voice vote of the Judiciary Committee's Crime Subcommittee two days after Columbine. The leadership sent it directly to the floor, thus bypassing the full Judiciary Committee. The second was H.R. 2122 and it would be the battleground for the more controversial gun control amendments. This bill bypassed all Judiciary Committee action and went straight to the floor.

The two key amendments to H.R. 2122 were by Representative Carolyn McCarthy (D-N.Y.), who lost her husband in a shooting rampage on the New York City subway, and Representative John D. Dingell (D-Mich.). The McCarthy amendment was considered the more restrictive of the two. It would have required background checks for potential buyers at gun shows and allowed three business days to complete the checks. Republicans generally contended that it was too broadly written and might put gun shows out of business. The amendment failed 235–193, and not even an emotional plea from the floor by McCarthy was enough to sway the House. She said in part:

> We have an opportunity here in Washington to stop playing games. That is what I came to Washington for. I am sorry that this is very hard for me. I am Irish, and I am not supposed to cry in front of anyone. But I made a promise a long time ago. I made a promise to my son and to my husband. If there was anything that I could do to prevent one family from going through what I have gone through and every other victim that I know have gone through, then I have done my job.[55]

Democrats were shocked when one of their own, Representative Dingell, teamed up with majority whip DeLay to introduce a gun control amendment that ultimately passed. It was unexpected for a Democrat to publicly work with the Republicans on such a controversial issue, even a Democrat who consistently opposed gun control throughout his career.

The Dingell amendment also required a background check, but one that must be completed within twenty-four hours. Many Democrats argued this was not enough time to conduct checks in all cases, as about one-quarter of all Brady Bill checks require more than one day. It was approved 218–211, with 45 Democrats in support and 47 Republicans opposed. Some Democrats afterwards spoke of denying Dingell the chair of the coveted Commerce Committee should the Democrats regain the majority in 2000, but such talk was largely in the heat of the moment.

The two alternative bills provided a choice for members, which they do not always receive. The House leadership, regardless of party, sometimes provides only one option, which members may reluctantly support given the lack of any other way to address the problem at hand. If the McCarthy amendment had been offered alone, it may well have passed, given the momentum from the Senate and public outrage over Columbine. The Dingell alternative allowed members to vote for a less restrictive gun control law, but nevertheless a gun control law. This would give them some political cover when questioned by gun control supporters in the next election. When questioned by gun owners, however, they could point out that the NRA supported the amendment, albeit reluctantly.

The question on many minds was whether Dingell was disloyal to his party or was trying to save the party from itself. Gun control may be generally popular in the Democratic Caucus, but it is much less so for members representing rural and conservative districts. If the Democratic effort to take back the House in 2000 was to have a chance at success, it could not comfortably rely on strong showings in liberal and urban districts. Although denounced by many, Dingell may have given Democrats in marginal districts a chance to vote on a hot-button issue in a manner acceptable to their constituents.

Many House members were put in a difficult position by the gun control votes. Democrats remembered the assault rifle bill in 1994, which was widely believed to have ended the careers of some Democratic proponents in the subsequent election. Representative James C. Greenwood (R-Pa.) noted that "A lot of Democrats think they can take back the Congress on guns,"[56] but at a Democratic Caucus meeting on May 25, the leadership warned that pushing too hard for tight gun control restrictions might endanger the 2000 election effort. Representative James P. Moran (D-Va.) estimated that gun control could be a problem in a dozen Democratic seats.[57]

Republicans, especially those from suburban districts, had their own problems. Representative Marge Roukema (R-N.J.) worried that the party could lose suburban female voters if it opposed gun restrictions: "In the last campaign, we talked about the Soccer Moms. This kind of issue is really relevant with women voters of all ages, not just Soccer Moms."[58] Republicans had long wanted to narrow the gender gap, and some feared this issue would only aggravate it.

With the addition of the Dingell amendment, H.R. 2122 was defeated 280–147. This was largely the result of Democrats who thought the bill was too weak, although a smaller group of Republicans who thought it went too far voted no.

The blame game was a key part of this debate. Many Democrats hoped that if they could not pass the McCarthy legislation they could at least blame the Republicans for its failure. The Dingell maneuver threw some doubt on the utility of the strategy, but in the end some Democratic unity was recovered as Dingell, McCarthy, and almost all Democrats voted against the final bill. As Representative Patrick J. Kennedy (D-R.I.) noted, "I was worried that Dingell was going to mix our message up." Who did he think should ultimately be blamed? "They're the majority. They're the ones who are going to get most hurt by this."[59] The Democrats also wanted to portray the Republicans as in the pocket of the NRA. President Clinton, traveling in Germany, said: "One more time, the Congress of the United States said, 'We don't care what's necessary to protect our children. We can't possibly bear to make anyone in the NRA mad.'"[60]

Republicans saw it otherwise. Speaker Hastert blamed the defeat on Democrats "who put partisanship over progress."[61] Referring to the Democrats, DeLay said, "The bill had four or five things they wanted [and] still was not good enough for them. So it's quite obvious to me that they're just interested in politics."[62] And Democrats could not complain that the Republicans had used procedural maneuvers to defeat them, as Hastert gave members two different gun show votes.

Forty-four amendments were considered for H.R. 1501, the second and less controversial Juvenile Justice bill considered by the House. They mostly dealt with criminal justice issues, the entertainment industry, and other issues not directly related to gun control. The underlying bill consisted of $1.5 billion for states to combat juvenile crime as they deemed best.[63] The more prominent amendments addressed the argument that changing the culture was more important than changing the criminal code. A condemnation of the entertainment industry for gratuitous violence, introduced by Representative Jo Ann Emerson (R-Mo.), passed by a voice vote. An amendment introduced by Representative Robert B. Aderholt (R-Ala.) to allow the Ten Commandments to be displayed on state and federal property also passed by a large margin. An amendment offered by Representative Zach Wamp (R-Tenn.) to create a uniform rating system for television, music videos, and other entertainment products was defeated, however.

The amendment Harkin attempted to filibuster in the Senate made an appearance in the House. Representative Charlie Norwood (R-Ga.) introduced an amendment allowing schools to discipline special education students the same way they would any other student if they bring a weapon or drugs to school. It passed by a large margin.

In the end, H.R. 1501 passed with 287 yeas and 139 nays. Because of this, a conference committee could be appointed to work out a compromise between the Senate and House bills. In the Senate, former Senator Robert C. Smith (R-N.H.), who at the time was running for president as an independent, attempted to filibuster several procedural matters in order to prevent Senate appointment of conferees. The effort failed when a cloture vote passed 77–22 and even Senator Larry Craig said "I see no reason to burn up the good will of the Senate by demanding vote after vote."[64] Speaker Hastert promised to name conferees for weeks but only did so on July 30, a day after a day trader in Atlanta allegedly killed his family as well as nine people at two brokerage firms before killing himself.

The most important conference issue was whether any gun control provisions would be included. Chairmen Hyde and Hatch said new restrictions were inevitable although compromise was necessary because the Senate gun show provision was unlikely to pass the House. According to Hatch, "We have an obligation to defend our institutions' respective positions. More importantly, we have an obligation to reconcile these firearms-related provisions in this conference."[65] Senator Schumer, however, threatened to filibuster the conference report if it weakened the Senate gun control provisions. The House approved by 305–84 a nonbinding motion to instruct its conferees to include some gun show language, but it was not clear what would be acceptable.

CONCLUSION

Gun control is one of the most difficult issues Congress considers. As Representative Jack Kingston (R-Ga.) said, "They say Social Security is the third rail of politics. They haven't been in a gun control debate."[66] Gun control involves strong emotions, partisan splits, powerful interests, and constitutional questions. Rural representatives are pitted against urban representatives, and suburban members are often caught in the middle. Although many members would prefer to never see another gun control vote in their lives, the late Representative Mike Synar (D-Okla.) once pointed out, "If you don't like fighting fires, don't be a fireman . . . and if you don't like voting, don't be a congressman."[67]

This episode featured a number of noteworthy procedural maneuvers. Some were examples of unorthodox lawmaking, which refers to deviations from the textbook description of how a bill becomes a law. In both the House and the Senate the underlying bills were moved out of committee and directly to the floor by the leadership. While this speeded up the process and gave the leadership more control, it also bypassed committee hearings and "the disadvantage is you don't have the education process," as former Representative Asa Hutchinson (R-Ark.) noted.[68]

The filibuster by Harkin might have been unusual several decades ago, but today delaying actions are relatively common. Cloture motions are now frequently filed, although the threat of a filibuster or a hold is more common than actual filibustering on the floor. In this case cloture was not necessary because Harkin and the Senate leadership were able to work out an arrangement.

There were also some events that were unusual even in an era of unorthodox lawmaking. The tie vote by Al Gore was only the fourth in his vice presidential career and gave his campaign for the Democratic presidential nomination some useful publicity. The amendment he pushed over the top, the Lautenberg gun show amendment, had been defeated only days before. In addition, two bills were passed that had been defeated in the previous year.

Despite this effort on the Senate side, it all came to naught because the House did not approve some of the amendments it adopted. The conference committee met only once and never crafted a compromise between the House and Senate versions, so the controversial provisions discussed earlier (such as the new gun-control measures) were not enacted into law. This illustrates how the bicameral nature of the institutional is not just an easily overlooked textbook description but a real obstacle to passing laws. Both sides must agree, and without agreement the long weeks of debating, negotiating, and voting in both chambers may just be sound and fury, signifying nothing.

NOTES

1. The vice president is automatically the president of the Senate and has an office near the Senate floor. This is a largely ceremonial position, however, and the only power of the office is breaking tie votes.
2. Barbara Sinclair, *Unorthodox Lawmaking: New Legislative Processes in the U.S. Congress* (Washington, D.C.: CQ Press, 1997).
3. *National Journal*, "How Congress Works: Not Always by the Book," May 13, 1999: 1297.
4. See Christopher J. Deering and Steven S. Smith, *Committees in Congress*, 2nd ed. (Washington, D.C.: CQ Press, 1997).
5. Woodrow Wilson, *Congressional Government* (Boston, MA: Houghton Mifflin, 1885).
6. Walter J. Oleszek, *Congressional Procedures and the Policy Process*, 4th ed. (Washington, D.C.: CQ Press, 1996). See Chapter 5.
7. Under this special rule, a number of major alternative amendments—each the functional equivalent of a bill—are made in order to the underlying measure, with the proviso that the substitute that garners the most votes is the winner. See Roger H. Davidson and Walter J. Oleszek, *Congress and Its Members*, 7th ed. (Washington, D.C.: CQ Press, 2000), p. 241.
8. Barbara Sinclair, *Unorthodox Lawmaking: New Legislative Processes in the U.S. Congress*, p. 31.
9. Ibid., p. 31.
10. *Congressional Record*, 13 May 1999: S5222.
11. Dan Carney, "Juvenile Crime Bill Heads Straight to the Senate Floor and a Battle over Gun Control," *Congressional Quarterly Weekly Report*, 8 May 1999: 1088.
12. Dan Carney, "Lott, Other Gun Control Foes on Defensive in Aftermath of Colorado School Killings," *Congressional Quarterly Weekly Report*, 1 May 1999: 1028.
13. Gerald Strom and Barry Rundquist, "A Revised Theory of Winning in House-Senate Conferences," *American Political Science Review* 71 (1977): 448–453.
14. Carney, "Lott, Other Gun Control Foes on Defensive in Aftermath of Colorado School Killings."
15. Dan Carney, "Seesaw Struggle over Gun Control Imperils Senate's Juvenile Crime Bill," *Congressional Quarterly Weekly Report*, 15 May 1999: 1142–1147.
16. *Congressional Record*, 19 May 1999: S5539.
17. Carney, "Seesaw Struggle over Gun Control Imperils Senate's Juvenile Crime Bill," p. 1142.
18. Ibid., pp. 1142–1143.
19. Helen Dewar and Roberto Suro, "Senate GOP Shifting on Gun Control; After Uproar, Leaders Endorse Background Checks at Shows," *Washington Post*, 14 May 1999, p. A1.
20. Dan Carney, "Seesaw Struggle over Gun Control Imperils Senate's Juvenile Crime Bill," p. 1142.
21. Ibid.
22. Ibid., p. 1143.
23. William Schneider, "Kids with Guns Riddle the NRA," *National Journal*, 29 May 1999: 1498.
24. Ibid.
25. Carroll Doherty, "Lott's Tactics Come under Fire after Gun Control Vote," *Congressional Quarterly Weekly Report*, 22 May 1999: 1206.

26. Quotation and discussion from Barbara Sinclair, *Unorthodox Lawmaking: New Legislative Processes in the U.S. Congress*, pp. 106–107.
27. Sarah Binder, *Minority Rights, Majority Rule* (Cambridge, UK: Cambridge University Press, 1998).
28. Barbara Sinclair, *Unorthodox Lawmaking: New Legislative Processes in the U.S. Congress*, p. 48.
29. Ibid.
30. In one of the most unusual stories from the 2000 election, Republican Senator John Ashcroft would lose his seat to a deceased challenger. His Democratic opponent, Missouri Governor Mel Carnahan, was killed in a small-airplane crash while campaigning, but his name remained on the ballot. The late Governor Carnahan garnered more votes on election day, and the new governor of Missouri appointed his widow to the Senate seat.
31. *Congressional Record*, 19 May 1999: S5540.
32. *Congressional Record*, 19 May 1999: S5542.
33. *Congressional Record*, 19 May 1999: S5548.
34. *Congressional Record*, 19 May 1999: S5542.
35. Oleszek, *Congressional Procedures and the Policy Process*.
36. *Congressional Record*, 20 May 1999: S5683.
37. Ibid.
38. Sinclair, *Unorthodox Lawmaking: New Legislative Processes in the U.S. Congress*, p. 49. Sinclair also notes that the only items that lost at the final stage in recent years were constitutional amendments, which require a two-thirds vote of the Senate.
39. Dan Carney, "Gun Control Backers Get Upper Hand as Senate Passes New Restrictions," *Congressional Quarterly Weekly Report*, 22 May 1999: 1204–1207.
40. Jack Germond and Jules Witcover, "Under Fire as Never Before," *National Journal*, 29 May 1999: 1492.
41. Doherty, "Lott's Tactics Come under Fire after Gun Control Vote."
42. Carney, "*Gun Control Backers Get Upper Hand as Senate Passes New Restrictions.*" Italics in original.
43. Carroll Doherty, "Lott's Tactics Come under Fire after Gun Control Vote."
44. Ibid.
45. Carney, "Gun Control Backers Get Upper Hand as Senate Passes New Restrictions."
46. Gebe Martinez, "GOP's Abiding Distrust of Clinton Doesn't Stop at Water's Edge," *Congressional Quarterly Weekly Report*, 1 May 1999: 1038–1039.
47. House Republicans wrote the juvenile crime bills of 1997 and 1999 without any reference to the criminal code, which would therefore make non-germane any Democratic amendments on gun control (Carney 1999e, p. 1204).
48. Dan Carney, "Hastert's Gun Control Package Faces Fusillade of Criticism from Both Parties," *Congressional Quarterly Weekly Report*, 12 June 1999: 1371–1373.
49. Ibid., p. 1372.
50. Peter Stone and David Byrd, "Will the NRA Hit Its Target?" *National Journal* 5 June 1999: 1336–1337.
51. Peter Stone, "Ready, Aim, Fire." *National Journal*, 15 May 1999: 1348.
52. *Congressional Record*, 20 May 1999: S5637.
53. *Congressional Record*, 13 May 1999: S5227. Hatch also provides in that speech statistics of Department of Justice (DOJ) prosecutions for violations of federal gun laws.
54. Jackie Koszczuk and Julie Hirschfeld, "Dreier Steers Gun Bill around Rules Pitfalls," *Congressional Quarterly Weekly Report*, 19 June 1999: 1425.
55. *Congressional Record*, 17 June 1999: H4605.
56. Dan Carney, "Beyond Guns and Violence: A Battle for House Control," *Congressional Quarterly Weekly Report*, 19 June 1999: 1426–1432.
57. Eliza Newlin Carney, "Caught in a Barrage over Gun Control," *National Journal*, 5 June 1999: 1534–1535.
58. Ibid.
59. Gebe Martinez, "Democrats' Frantic Maneuvering Ultimately Comes to Naught," *Congressional Quarterly Weekly Report*, 19 June 1999: 1430–1431.
60. Carney, "Beyond Guns and Violence: A Battle for House Control," p. 1426.
61. Ibid., p. 1427.
62. Ibid.

63. The measure reauthorized the Juvenile Accountability Block Grants, which received $250 million in fiscal year (FY) 1999.
64. Dan Carney, "House Names Negotiators, but Juvenile Crime Bill Will Lag New School Year," *Congressional Quarterly Weekly Report*, 31 July 1999: 1874. See also Richard Cohen, "A Fork in the Democratic Road to 2000," *National Journal*, 26 June 1999: 1894–1895.
65. Dan Carney, "Juvenile Crime Bill Conferees Begin Quest for Agreement on Gun Control Proposals," *Congressional Quarterly Weekly Report*, 7 August 1999: 1944.
66. Carney, "Hastert's Gun Control Package Faces Fusillade of Criticism from Both Parties," p. 1372.
67. Jack Anderson and Michael Binstein. "Synar Stands His Ground," *Washington Post*, 22 August 1993, C7.
68. Carney, "Beyond Guns and Violence: A Battle for House Control," p. 1373.

5

A DIFFICULT HABIT TO KICK

THE DEFEAT OF THE UNIVERSAL TOBACCO SETTLEMENT ACT

CHRISTOPHER J. BAILEY

Passage of a major antismoking bill seemed inevitable in the spring of 1998. Few doubted that bipartisan legislation (S. 1415) sponsored by Senator John McCain (R-Ariz.) to codify a 1997 settlement between the tobacco industry and forty states had the support of a majority in the Senate. "I would be very surprised, ultimately, if this legislation didn't pass with a strong majority in the end" commented cosponsor Senator John F. Kerry (D-Mass.) in April 1998.[1] A few weeks later, on the eve of floor debate, a veteran lobbyist posed the question: "Who dares vote against it? I think the thing passes 80 to 20."[2] Even opponents of the bill seemed resigned to its passage. "I don't think the votes are there to sustain a filibuster" remarked Senator Mitch McConnell (R-Ky.).[3] In less than a month, however, such predictions proved inaccurate. On June 17, 1998, a fourth attempt to invoke cloture failed to achieve the required sixty votes, and the legislation was lost when supporters failed to muster the votes needed to overcome a point of order challenge to the bill.

The rise and fall of S. 1415 affords a wonderful opportunity to examine the cut and thrust of legislative politics in the Senate. All the major ingredients of a "war story" *par excellence* are present. Not only does the "story" offer important insights into the ability of the Senate to legislate on a complex and "unbounded" issue, but it also highlights many key and controversial elements of legislative politics.[4] It includes a crucial struggle to define the terms of debate, a legislative battlefield awash with millions of dollars, procedural battles on the floor of the Senate, and defeat of a bill supported by a majority of senators, the president, and probably most Americans. Legislative scholars, policy analysts, and practitioners will find important lessons about bill drafting, coalition building, political rhetoric, interest group influence, and procedural maneuvers in the story of S. 1415.

"WHERE THERE'S SMOKE, THERE'S FIRE":
THE POLITICS OF AGENDA-SETTING

On November 7, 1997, Senator McCain, chair of the Senate Committee on Commerce, Science, and Transportation took the floor of the Senate during Morning Hour. Known in Congress primarily for his high-minded legislative failures, particularly his efforts to reform campaign finance, the Arizonan had been selected by the Republican leadership in the Senate to reform regulation of the tobacco industry. "Mr. President, I am pleased today to introduce the Universal Tobacco Settlement Act (S. 1415). This bill is cosponsored by the Commerce Committee Ranking Member Senator Hollings, Senator Gorton, and Senator Breaux," McCain told the customary near-empty chamber.[5] "Mr. President, the bill we are introducing today is the legislative version of the Universal Tobacco Settlement agreed upon by the attorneys general and the tobacco companies," he continued, "We hope it will serve as the basis of discussion and amendment here in the Senate." McCain admitted that "The substance of the bill is not perfect, complete, comprehensive, or legislation that could ever be signed into law without considerable debate and amendments," but claimed that "it can and should serve as a basis to begin negotiations between all concerned parties."

The major tobacco companies and forty-one states signed the Universal Tobacco Settlement on June 20, 1997, between forty states to settle a range of state and other civil suits against the industry.[6] The settlement required Big Tobacco to pay the states $368 billion over twenty-five years to offset some of the medical costs associated with smoking-related illness, submit to Food and Drug Administration (FDA) regulation, agree to some restrictions on advertising and marketing, and agree to meet youth tobacco use reduction targets. In return, the tobacco industry received some protection from further litigation. The grant of limited liability, changes in the regulatory authority of the FDA, and advertising restrictions contained in the Settlement required congressional approval before they could take effect, but few involved in the negotiations that had led to the agreement of June 20, 1997, believed that there would be problems in passing the appropriate implementing legislation. Industry executives believed that President Clinton would endorse the deal within days, and that Congress would act quickly to ratify it. Few paid much heed to then-House Speaker Newt Gingrich's comment on the day after the Settlement was announced that, "The Constitution does not make any provision for Congress to delegate to private groups in secret meetings the power to write the laws."[7]

Speaker Gingrich's caustic remark reflected a feeling of cynicism in Congress toward the tobacco industry that structured the early politics surrounding the Settlement. Growing public concern about underage smoking, and new evidence that Big Tobacco had engaged in unsavory business practices had "demonized" the industry to such an extent that most politicians sought to distance themselves from the likes of Joe Camel and Marlboro Man.

Few were willing to stand up and support an industry that had been charged with smuggling cigarettes into Canada, committing perjury in congressional committee hearings, engaging in antitrust activities, and promoting what Dr. John Seffrin, CEO of the American Cancer Society, termed a "pediatric epidemic" of underage smoking.[8] Even traditional allies of the industry such as Representative Thomas J. Bliley (R-Va.), dubbed "R-Philip Morris" for his support of his hometown industry, told industry representatives that he no longer had much "confidence that your companies care about the truth."

Antipathy toward Big Tobacco meant that the Settlement did not receive the endorsements that industry executives expected. President Clinton treated news of the agreement with caution. At a press conference in Denver on June 20, 1997, he stated that he needed "to subject the proposed agreement to strict scrutiny . . . [and] would judge this agreement based on whether it advances the public health and will reduce the number of children who are smoking cigarettes."[9] Clinton appointed Domestic Policy Advisor Bruce Reed and Health and Human Services (HHS) director Donna Shalala to head a team that would review the Settlement and report back "in a matter of weeks." The review did not result in a simple endorsement of the Settlement. On September 17, 1997, President Clinton told members of Congress, state attorneys general, and private plaintiffs gathered in the Oval Office that "we have this unprecedented opportunity to enact comprehensive tobacco legislation."[10] He challenged Congress to enact "sweeping legislation that has one goal in mind: the dramatic reduction of teen smoking," and identified "five key elements that must be at the heart of any national tobacco legislation." Legislation should increase the tax on cigarettes, confirm the full authority of the FDA to regulate tobacco products, include measures to hold the tobacco industry accountable for its activities, contain provisions to reduce smoking in the general population, and protect tobacco farmers from loss of income.

President Clinton's reaction to the Universal Tobacco Settlement of June 20, 1997, shaped the politics surrounding the issue in two important ways. First, he successfully changed the terms of debate. Clinton portrayed the Settlement as something to build upon to protect the lives of children rather than a carefully crafted compromise between the states and Big Tobacco.[11] Framing the issue in this way palliated some of the traditional arguments employed to defend smoking, but promised to engender conflict with the tobacco industry. President Clinton conspicuously failed to invite any representatives of the industry to the Oval Office when he announced his plans on September 17, 1997, and offered only begrudging acknowledgement of their willingness to broker a deal. Second, no offer to submit legislation to Congress was made. President Clinton detailed the key elements he believed should be contained within a bill, talked about his wish to work with Congress on the issue, but offered no legislative language of his own. This left members of Congress with the task of drafting legislation that conformed with the president's aims but retained the central features of the Settlement.

Senator McCain noted the administration's failure to submit legislation to Congress when he introduced S. 1415 on November 7, 1997. McCain stated: "I had hoped that the administration would send the Congress legislation in this area. I would have liked for the Congress to begin considering the proposals developed and advocated by the White House."[12] In the absence of such legislation, McCain claimed that he had decided to use the Universal Tobacco Settlement "to move the legislative process forward and begin debating substantive language." "[L]et me emphasize that this legislation was drafted by Senate legislative counsel who was requested to write a bill that would implement and mirror the universal tobacco agreement without any direction or input from Members and without any alteration from the agreement," he declared. The bill "is the basis for hearings, discussion, and amendment," he continued, "I intend to hold extensive hearings on this bill and use it as a vehicle for amendment." This strategy departed from usual custom. Normally, authors of significant and controversial bills seek to iron out differences in the privacy of congressional offices. McCain proposed to do the "dirty work" in public.

The magnitude of the task confronting Senator McCain became apparent when the Commerce Committee began to conduct hearings on S. 1415. The committee held seven hearings between February 24, 1998, and March 23, 1998, and thirty-seven different witnesses gave evidence.[13] A measure of how successfully opponents of the tobacco industry had framed the debate in the period since the Settlement had been announced can be seen in the testimony given to the committee. Only eight of the witnesses spoke unambiguously in favor of the Settlement: the chairmen of the five major tobacco companies, a representative of the smokeless tobacco products industry, Attorney General Carla Stovall of Kansas, and former senator Connie Mack (R-Fla.). The other witnesses articulated a range of concerns. Administration officials and health groups argued that the regulatory authority of the FDA had to be strengthened, cigarette taxes needed to be increased, the provisions concerning industry liability had to be clarified, and Big Tobacco needed to do more to limit underage smoking. Considerable debate centered on whether the proposed advertising restrictions in the legislation would survive constitutional challenges, and experts from Wall Street discussed the financial effects of the Settlement on the tobacco industry.

Pressure for legislation that moved beyond the Tobacco Settlement had become considerable by the spring of 1998. Geoffrey Bible, chairman and CEO of Philip Morris, received a frosty reception when he visited the mahogany-paneled office of Senate Majority Whip Don Nickles (R-Okla.) to seek support for the original agreement. "This isn't last June; this is February 1998 and things aren't going well for you," Nickles said, "You are not going to get what you're looking for here."[14] Republicans feared that they would be portrayed as friends of a "demonized" industry in an election year if they failed to enact tough antismoking legislation. Vice President Al Gore had already sought to take political advantage of the issue by visiting Capitol Hill to remind legislators that "support for tough antitobacco measures crosses all lines of region, party, and politics."[15] Past campaign contributions from the tobacco industry appeared especially worrying to Republicans. Big tobacco had contributed generously to Republican coffers in the 1990s and members feared that such contributions would haunt them at the ballot box if they were seen to support the industry. "Members are afraid of the taint of that money," stated one Republican aide, "There's a race to see who can punish the industry more."[16] Speaker Gingrich put the matter even more bluntly when he told a group of tobacco lobbyists: "You guys have screwed us. The Republican Party has been saddled with tobacco."[17]

Pressure for tough antismoking legislation led to ten days of tense negotiations as McCain sought to fashion a substitute amendment acceptable to colleagues on the Commerce Committee. On the morning of March 25 he struggled to control his rage when two of his staff told him that disagreement about how much authority the FDA should have to regulate tobacco products threatened to torpedo negotiations.[18] Clutching the back of a chair in his office he shouted "OK, what? What?" before regaining his composure. He looked at the rubber band that he always kept around his right wrist and calmly told the staff, "It's OK. We knew this was going to happen." Then he repeated a mantra that had helped him survive five and a half years as a POW in Hanoi: "Remember, steady strain. You gotta keep a steady strain." McCain had his composure tested again the following night when a committee staffer working for the majority kicked over a chair to vent his frustration at Democratic efforts to remove the legal immunity granted to tobacco companies in the bill. McCain phoned Senator John Kerry (D-Mass.), a fellow Vietnam veteran, to apologize for the staff member's actions. "I'm deeply embarrassed," he told the senator from Massachusetts, "You do play an important role." He then reminded his staff of a basic rule of legislative politics: "Look, if John's not in on the takeoff of this thing, he won't be in on the landing."

Senator McCain's efforts to keep everyone on board finally paid off on April 1, 1998, when the Commerce Committee voted 19–1 for a substitute amendment that strengthened S. 1415. Although the legislation reported by the Committee had the same structural framework as the Tobacco Settlement, it differed from the original bill in a number of important areas. The amount that the tobacco industry had to pay the states to settle outstanding legal suits was increased from $368 billion to $516 billion over twenty-five years, the penalties that Big Tobacco would have to pay if targets for reducing underage smoking were not achieved (so-called "look-backs") were almost doubled, and, perhaps most significantly, the authority of the FDA to regulate nicotine and tobacco products was strengthened. Drafted by Senator Bill Frist (R-Tenn.), a former heart surgeon, the section dealing with FDA regulatory authority revealed just how strong antismoking sentiment was on Capitol Hill in spring 1998. Republicans were willing to give an agency that ranked second only to the Internal Revenue Service in their pantheon of bureaucratic *betes noirs* sweeping new powers to ban nicotine after a two-year period of grace. The legislation gave the industry an annual civil liability cap of $6.5 billion, but failed to give it immunity from litigation by groups or individuals.

The tobacco industry greeted the Commerce Committee's version of S. 1415 with dismay and promised to fight the legislation. R. J. Reynolds' Chief Executive Officer Steven F. Goldstone stated that tobacco politics is "broken beyond repair. There is no process which is even remotely likely to lead to an acceptable comprehensive solution this year."[19] Similar announcements from the other major tobacco companies signaled an end to the industry's strategy of working with Congress, the White House, and the states to reach a national tobacco settlement. Goldstone declared that the industry would devote resources to fighting the McCain bill by taking its case to the American public, and would return to a combative stance in the courtroom. Most of those involved in drafting S. 1415 greeted news of the industry's announcements with regret but promised to continue without Big Tobacco's cooperation. Vice President Gore issued a statement that expressed disappointment about "R. J. Reynolds' decision to walk away from our efforts to reduce underage smoking," but confirmed that the administration "will continue our efforts to reduce youth smoking, and to pass a comprehensive, bipartisan bill this year."[20] Senator McCain stated that Congress must proceed "with or without the industry's support . . . we could never be placed in a position where the terms of this agreement are dictated."[21] Senator Kent Conrad (D-N.D.), a passionate antismoker, dismissed the walkout by the tobacco companies in more colorful language. "Poor babies," he jibed, "We don't need their blessing to pass tough tobacco legislation. In many ways this is liberating—do it right, and not try to dance around their approval. They weren't going to approve of anything that was any good anyway."[22] Others displayed greater caution in their prognosis. Former Senator Wendell H. Ford (D-Ky.), the most famous cigarette smoker in the Senate, argued that the industry's announcements would either "cause the legislative process to disintegrate" or "inject some needed fiscal responsibility into the debate."[23]

The potential for the "legislative process to disintegrate" had been evident in the Commerce Committee's consideration of S. 1415. Amendments had been offered during the Commerce Committee's mark-up of the bill that would have changed the substitute amendment in substantial ways. Former Senator John D. Ashcroft (R-Mo.) and Senator Byron L. Dorgan (D-N.D.) offered amendments to remove the liability cap, Senator Olympia J. Snowe (R-Maine) tried to codify provisions related to advertising and marketing, and former Senator Wendell H. Ford sought to reduce the sum that the tobacco industry would have to pay. Although Senator McCain managed to hold a core coalition of thirteen senators together to defeat all amendments bar one that required Indian tribes to collect state taxes on tobacco, the range and nature of the amendments suggested that strong efforts would be made to change the bill on the floor of the Senate. Senator Ron Wyden (D-Ore.) predicted that floor debate "will not be for the faint-hearted."[24] Few believed, however, that tough antismoking legislation would not be passed. "Anyone who thinks they're going to keep a tough tobacco bill from passing in the Senate isn't living in the real world," declared Senator Charles E. Grassley (R-Iowa).[25] The question simply seemed to be "how tough?"

EXHALING TOO SOON: THE DEFEAT OF S. 1415

The first sign that the floor debate on S. 1415 "[would] not be for the faint-hearted" came on May 13, 1998, when Senator William V. Roth (R-Del.), chair of the Finance Committee, asserted the right of his committee to examine the tax provisions contained in the bill by placing a "hold" on the legislation. The "hold" stopped the Senate from considering the bill. Majority Leader Lott agreed to refer S. 1415 to the Finance Committee to placate Roth, but insisted that the Committee had to report the bill by 9:00 P.M. the following day or it would be discharged.[26] Supporters of the legislation watched anxiously as Roth tried to use the $516 billion from the tobacco industry to finance new tax cuts. In a surprising rebuff, however, the Finance Committee voted 10–9 to raise the excise tax on cigarettes from $1.10 to $1.50 per pack. The committee subsequently approved the amended bill on a 13 to 6 vote, and reported it favourably on May 14, 1998. Roth voted against his committee's amendment because he believed that its tax bill was too high.

Proponents of strong antismoking legislation welcomed the Finance Committee's actions. They believed that the Committee's approval presaged enactment of tough legislation. "You saw what happened in the Finance Committee," crowed Senator Edward M. Kennedy (D-Mass.), "They can't vote against it."[27] Those involved in crafting the bill were more circumspect. Senator McCain stated, "I am functioning under the assumption, 'Take nothing for granted.' There's always the possibility this thing could be the exploding cigar."[28] Particularly worrying for McCain was the possibility that the increase in the cigarette excise tax could cost him the support of senators from tobacco farm states. Senator Ernest F. "Fritz" Hollings (D-S.C.), McCain's main cosponsor, had already threatened to oppose the bill if the tax raise voted by the Finance Committee was not reversed. He feared that tobacco farmers would suffer financially if a tax raise caused a dramatic decrease in cigarette consumption.

Senator Hollings expressed his concern about the plight of tobacco farmers when floor debate started in the Senate on May 18, 1998, in an episode that illustrates both the importance of parochial concerns and the parliamentary power of the majority. The ire of Senator Hollings had been raised when Majority Leader Lott announced "managers' amendments" to the bill that had been agreed to by the Republican majority on the Commerce Committee.

These amendments replaced provisions to protect tobacco farmers that Hollings had authored with new language written by Senator Richard G. "Dick" Lugar (R-Ind.), chair of the Agriculture Committee. Hollings, Commerce's ranking member, was incandescent. In an impassioned speech he stated that he had not been consulted about the changes, claiming "this kind of conduct and course of conduct is just the worst I have seen in my 30-some years up here."[29] "There is no question that if this so-called tobacco bill works, there can't be any tobacco farmer unless there are tobacco companies. This is going to diminish the tobacco companies to a great extent and limit the tobacco farmers, as they go down or out of business," he continued.[30] Senator Ford joined Hollings in condemning the bill. Ford told colleagues that, "I am going to make it as difficult as I can to see that this bill is not passed this week, and probably not in June. I believe my responsibility here is to the farmer. . . ."[31] Senator McCain took the floor in an effort to calm nerves. "This is a difficult situation and not the first that we have been through in this process, nor regrettably, I feel, will it be the last. I have great sympathy for my two dear friends—one from Kentucky, one from South Carolina—who fought very hard for the people they represent," he stated, "It was my understanding I would be managing this bill with the distinguished Senator from South Carolina. I will make every effort to make sure that fairness is the order of the day, which has been the way we have conducted our relationship and our negotiations throughout his bill."[32] He dismissed claims, however, that the majority had acted improperly and reminded the two Democrats that they employed similar parliamentary tactics when they were in the majority. Hollings responded by ceding the floor but warned that "bipartisanship is ended."[33]

The task facing Senator McCain as floor action loomed was to prevent the carefully crafted compromise bill that had been fashioned by the Commerce Committee from being unpicked on the floor. Senator Hollings's reaction to the increase in the cigarette excise tax voted by the Finance Committee revealed the fragility of the coalition in support of S. 1415. Ranged on one side were antismoking forces that wished to strengthen the bill. Senators Judd Gregg (R-N.H.) and Conrad promised to offer amendments that would remove the liability limits granted to the industry. Senator John H. Chafee (R-R.I.) wanted to add language to the bill that would ban smoking in federal buildings and on all international flights that landed in America. Others wished to weaken the bill. Senator Nickles wanted to reduce the cost and regulatory burden of the bill. Senator Orrin G. Hatch (R-Utah) sought to offer a substitute amendment modeled more closely on the original tobacco settlement of June 1997. "We are going to hear attacks," Senator McCain warned the Senate as debate began. "There are people waiting right now to attack this bill in the most vociferous and passionate fashion, and there are people on the other side who will say: You guys aren't tough enough on these tobacco companies; you've got to do more. . . . But

I believe the great center will hold on this bill, and I believe that a fair procedure will follow."[34] The problem confronting Senator McCain was that a single successful amendment might cause the whole package to unravel like a pulled thread in a sweater.

Senator McCain had been able to knit S. 1415 together because supporters of new legislation to regulate the tobacco industry had been able to frame the issue in "motherhood and apple pie" terms of protecting children's health. This had put the tobacco industry and its supporters in the difficult position of trying to defend something that virtually all Americans believed to be indefensible. The clarity of this message, however, had begun to fade by the time floor debate in the Senate started. For example, President Clinton had proposed in his fiscal 1999 budget to use money obtained from the tobacco industry to fund "feel-good proposals" for medical research, child-care, and new teachers.[35] Opponents of the legislation seized upon this dilution of the original message to develop a new rhetorical strategy that sought to frame the issue in different terms. Rather than contest claims about underage smoking or mortality rates among smokers, the tobacco industry and its allies focused upon the tax raises contained in S. 1415 and the cost of the legislation. The aim was to portray the bill as a "tax and spend" measure.

Huge tax increases to support a bloated government was the central message of an unprecedented $40 million, nine-week advertising campaign launched by the tobacco industry on April 18, 1998. In a broadcasting blitz that dwarfed the "Harry and Louise" campaign that had helped to defeat President Clinton's health care reforms in 1994, Big Tobacco purchased time in 30 to 50 television markets each week, ran commercials on CNN nationally for three weeks, and bought spots on local radio. One commercial even appeared in the final episode of the popular program *Seinfeld*. Three rounds of print advertisements in major national newspapers such as The *Washington Post* and *USA Today* accompanied this television blitz. All the commercials and advertisements hammered home the same message. A letter from the National Smokers Alliance sent to Republican leaders, 250 radio shows, and conservative opinion polls asked: "Are you ready for the largest middle-class tax increase in American history?" A typical television commercial showed a Christmas tree in front of the Capitol with a voice-over that told viewers: "It's the season of giving in Washington, but remember, it's your taxes they're giving away."

The impact of the advertising blitz launched by the tobacco industry has been disputed.[36] Opinion polls conducted for the White House and public health groups found little change in public support for increased regulation of the industry. A poll released by ENACT, a public health coalition, revealed that registered voters supported S. 1415 by a 2–1 margin. A poll by the nonpartisan Pew Research Center found similar support for government efforts to restrict the tobacco industry. Republican pollster Linda Divall, however, obtained a different result. She found that 69 percent of those polled believed that supporters of the tobacco bill were more interested in raising tax revenue than curbing underage smoking. Big Tobacco had managed to persuade a majority of the voting population that the "voluntary" $368 billion payment contained in the Tobacco Settlement of June 1998 had become a $516 billion tax to fund social programs wanted by President Clinton.

The tobacco industry launched a lobbying campaign unprecedented in its size and cost to promote its "tax-and-spend" message in Congress. A report by Public Citizen estimated that the industry spent more than $43 million on lobbying Congress in the first six months of 1998.[37] This was over three times the amount that the industry had spent in the first six months of 1997. Joan Claybrook, president of Public Citizen, claimed that these outlays "put the voice, the message and the pressure of the tobacco industry way ahead of the citizen."[38] Not only did the industry employ 192 lobbyists to do the rounds on Capitol Hill, but their message was promoted by a number of big-name Washington insiders. Among the lobbyists hired by Big Tobacco were at least eight former members of Congress including former Senate Majority Leaders George Mitchell (D-Maine) and Howard Baker (R-Tenn.), and former Senator Walter D. Huddleston (D-Ky.). At least twenty ex-congressional staff members also lobbied for the tobacco industry. A number of these ex-staffers had previously worked for members of Congress who were involved in crafting tobacco legislation.

Former members of Congress have proved to be some of the most effective lobbyists in Washington D.C. Not only do these former members have extensive knowledge of the legislative process, but more important, they invariably have close connections to current members. "We have access that a nonmember would not have," noted Senator Huddleston.[39] The access enjoyed by former members provides them with the means to have an input

TABLE 5.1   FORMER MEMBERS OF CONGRESS
WHO LOBBIED FOR THE TOBACCO INDUSTRY

NAME	EMPLOYER
George Mitchell (D-Maine)	Verner, Liipfert, Bernhard, McPherson & Hand
Howard Baker (R-Tenn.)	Baker, Donelson, Bearman & Caldwell
Walter D. Huddleston (D-Ky.)	Self-employed
Ed Jenkins (D-Ga.)	Winburn, Jenkins & Wheat
Alan Wheat (D-Mo.)	Winburn, Jenkins & Wheat
Ray Kogovsek (D-Colo.)	Black, Kelly, Scruggs & Healy
James V. Stanton (D-Ohio)	Stanton & Associates
Stanford Parris (R-Va.)	Dickstein, Shapiro, Morin & Oshinsky

Source: Public Citizen, "Burning Down the Houses," March 1998. Downloaded from <www.citizen.org/congress/civjus/tobacco/burning.htm>.

TABLE 5.2   TOBACCO LOBBYISTS WHO PREVIOUSLY
WORKED AS CONGRESSIONAL STAFFERS

NAME	CURRENT EMPLOYER	FORMERLY
Michael F. Barrett	Self-employed	Staff Director, House Commerce Cmte., Subcmte. on Oversight and Investigations
Elizabeth Beavin	Bergner, Bockorny, et al.	Leg. Asst., U.S. House of Reps.
Charles Brain	The White House	Dep. Staff Dir., Ways & Means Cmte.
John Doney	Washington Counsel, P.C.	Asst. Secretary for the Majority, Senate
Jayne T. Fitzgerald	Washington Counsel, P.C.	Tax Counsel, Ways & Means Cmte.
Ed Gillespie	Barbour, Griffiths, et al.	Aide, House Majority Leader Armey (R-TX-26)
G. Stewart Hall	G. Stewart Hall & Assoc.	Leg. Dir., Sen. Shelby (R-AL)
Rodney C. Hoppe	Oldaker, Ryan, et al.	Dep. Press Sec., House Commerce Cmte.
Keith Kennedy	Baker, Donelson, et al.	Staff Dir., Senate Appropriations Cmte.
Graham Matthews	Dickstein, Shapiro, et al.	Minority Clerk, Senate Appropriations Cmte.
Richard Meltzer	Washington Counsel, P.C.	Chief Counsel, Natural Resources Cmte.
James T. Molloy	Self-employed	Doorkeeper, U.S. House of Reps.
Darryl D. Nirenberg	Patton Boggs	Chief of Staff, Sen. Helms (R-NC)
William Nordwind	O'Connor & Hannan	Leg. Asst., Rep. Upton (R-MI-6)
Steven R. Phillips	Verner, Liipfert, et al.	Leg. Director, Sen. Helms (R-NC)
Karen A. Regan	Oldaker, Ryan, et al.	Leg. Asst., House Admin. Cmte.
Jeffrey Schlagenhauf	Smokeless Tobacco	Aide, Rep. Bliley (R-VA-7)
Thomas Spulak	Shaw, Pittman, et al.	General Counsel, U.S. House of Reps.
Jessica Wallace	Verner, Liipfert, et al.	Leg. Council, Rep. Stearns (R-FL-6)
Mark Weinberger	Washington Counsel, P.C.	Chief of Staff, Comm. on Entitlement and Tax Reform (Exec. Branch)

Source: Public Citizen, "Burning Down the Houses," March 1998. Downloaded from
<www.citizen.org/congress/civjus/tobacco/burning.htm>.

into the legislative process that is difficult for other lobbyists to match. Huddleston's value as a tobacco lobbyist, for example, derived from his good relationship with senators from tobacco-growing states, such as fellow Kentuckian Wendell Ford and South Carolinian Earnest Hollings. Former staff members also have considerable value as lobbyists. Like former members, they have detailed knowledge of the legislative process, and usually have considerable contacts among current congressional staff. The contacts of John Doney, G. Stewart Hall, Keith Kennedy, Daryl Nirenberg, and Steven Phillips allowed them to put the views of the tobacco industry to staff members working on S. 1415.

Big tobacco's advertising and lobbying campaign not only provided opponents of S. 1415 with a rhetoric to frame the issue in favourable terms, but also served to embolden them. Speaker Gingrich took the lead in a letter to colleagues in which he claimed that: "The American people see through the president's thinly veiled effort to use massive tobacco taxes to pay for his liberal agenda of new government programs, more spending and bigger bureaucracy."[40] Gingrich's message that smoking was bad but increased taxes and big government were even worse provided a mantra that Republican opponents of the legislation could coalesce behind. Rather than be cast as supporters of underage smoking, opponents could argue that they were seeking to defend the American taxpayer from higher taxes and more bureaucracy. Archconservative Senator Phil Gramm (R-Texas), for example, described the legislation as a "Big Brother" bill that "had no support in America."[41]

Supporters of the legislation recognized the threat posed by framing S. 1415 as a "tax-and-spend" bill. President Clinton complained that the tobacco industry's campaign was designed to "channel [voters] well-known hatred of government and taxes against this bill."[42] In an effort to shift debate back to the "children's health" frame that had proved unassailable earlier in the year, Clinton held a photo-opportunity on the South Lawn of the White House on May 20, 1998. Addressing 1,400 children from local schools, he stated that "Our lawmakers must not let this historic opportunity slip away under pressure from big tobacco lobbying," and told the children, "I know you're going to Capitol Hill—when you're up there, I want you to ask every member of Congress to go home tonight and think about how they can look you in the eye and say no to your future."[43] Senator McCain also sought to address the "tax-and-spend" issue head-on at the beginning of floor debate in the Senate. He told colleagues, "Now because the industry fears that the bill may actually achieve what it purports to, the effort has been transmuted from enlightened public policy to tax and spend Government."[44] "If this bill is killed," McCain continued, "the ultimate prices in cigarettes will be little different from what might result from this bill, but we will pay an awful price in terms of the 3,000 children a day who will become regular users of tobacco and consign themselves to the consequences before they are adult enough to make that life or death decision."

The efforts of President Clinton and Senator McCain to refocus attention on the issue of underage smoking came too late. Big Tobacco's advertising and lobbying campaign, Clinton's willingness to use tobacco payments to fund government programs, and the media's preoccupation with the emerging Monica Lewinsky scandal had undermined the ability of the bill's supporters to control the terms of debate. Just a couple of hours after the president had made his plea on the South Lawn of the White House, the difficulties facing S. 1415's sponsors became apparent when Senator Ashcroft rose to speak. "Mr President, along with my colleagues, I am truly concerned about teen smoking," he began, "However, I do not believe that is the focus of this legislation. Teen smoking is not the central thrust of what is happening here."[45] Articulating the "tax-and-spend" message of the industry's commercials, Ashcroft asserted that: "This is an $868 billion—that is not million, that is billion—tax increase. It creates Government programs . . . creates a huge Governmental regulatory scheme the likes of which we have not seen since the Clinton proposal to nationalize the health care system." The junior senator from Missouri offered an amendment (SP. 2427) to strike all the consumer taxes from S. 1415, but was defeated on a 72 to 26 vote.

Defeat of Senator Ashcroft's amendment caused opponents of S. 1415 to reassess legislative tactics as they realized that they did not have enough votes to kill or gut the bill. Some decided that the best chance of defeating the bill was to vote with liberal senators to make the measure unacceptable to the House of Representatives. A number of conservative Republicans voted with Democrats, for example, to pass amendments that eliminated the bill's cap on legal damages that tobacco companies could be forced to pay, and stiffened the "look-back" penalties on cigarette manufacturers who failed to reach goals for reducing youth smoking. Senator Robert G. Torricelli (D-N.J.) recognized this tactic. He observed that "the legislation is in some real trouble because the people who want no legislation at all are trying to make it so good that it becomes bad."[46] Others decided that sharing in the bonanza offered by the billions of dollars of tobacco money constituted the best tactic. Several conservative Republicans regarded the bill as offering an opportunity to advance pet causes such as drug use, school vouchers, and tax cuts.

Conservative Senators Paul Coverdell (R-Ga.) and Larry E. Craig (R-Idaho) combined the issues of drug use and school vouchers in a sweeping antidrugs amendment (SP. 2451). The amendment authorized $16 billion over five years to fund drug interdiction programs, boosted numbers of Custom Service border guards, banned the use of federal funds for needle exchange programs, restricted convicted drug criminals from receiving federal student loans, and created a community registration bank for drug dealers similar to the sex offender registry established by "Megan's Law." Most controversially, the amendment also allowed federal funds to be spent on school vouchers to allow children who have been victims of violent crime to attend private schools. Most Republicans strongly supported the amendment. "Mr President, I rise in support of Senator Coverdell's and Senator Craig's amendment. These two Senators have focused attention on a critical issue for the next generation of Americans," former Senator Lauch Faircloth (R-N.C.) informed the Senate.[47] "While tobacco use by teenagers is a problem, illegal drug use by teenagers is much more than a problem, it is a crisis. And if our mandate is to protect our Nation's children, then we must not ignore our illicit drug crisis," he continued. Democrats supported many of the provisions in the Coverdell-Craig amendment, but vehemently opposed the school voucher plan. Senator Kerry claimed that, "Provisions such as the voucher program have very little to do with drug fighting."[48] Democratic efforts to strip the Coverdell-Craig amendment of the voucher plan were defeated, however, and the amendment eventually passed on a 52–46 vote.

Senator Gramm made an effort to use tobacco money to finance tax cuts in an amendment that would abolish the so-called marriage tax penalty. Republicans had frequently criticized a provision of the tax law that forced some couples to pay higher taxes following marriage, and Gramm sought to exploit such sentiments to undermine S. 1415. His amendment (SP. 2686) sought to give a tax reduction to all married couples earning less than $50,000 per year, and to offer self-employed workers a 100 percent deduction for health insurance payments, at a total cost of $46 billion over five years. Democrats charged that the amendment would consume about 70 percent of the revenue generated by the bill over twenty-five years. Negotiations over the amendment slowed proceedings in the Senate to a snail's pace as quorum call followed quorum call while the bill's managers and Gramm sought to find a compromise. While the Clerk of the Senate wearily intoned senator's names, McCain harried Gramm in the corridors of the Senate to persuade him to reduce his demands. Eventually Gramm agreed to changes that reduced the cost of his amendment to $16.8 billion. Despite misgivings among several Republicans, the amendment passed by voice vote on June 10, 1998, after a motion to table it had failed 48–50. Senator Hatch, who had previously argued that S. 1415 was not the vehicle to address the marriage tax penalty, voted against the motion to table because he believed the bill had "become an absolute mess . . . and I'm not going to vote against the marriage penalty tax."[49]

The observation that S. 1415 had "become an absolute mess" was essentially correct. Amendments adopted during floor debate had blurred the focus of the bill to such an extent that it resembled a beached whale. "I think it is critical that we remain focused on the smoking-related aspects of this legislation, rather than some of the other attempts to sort of grab some of the revenue and use it for worthy but nevertheless non-related causes," Senator

Kerry pleaded with colleagues.[50] Kerry's plea, however, went unnoticed. More than 250 amendments remained pending as debate entered its fourth week and opponents showed little willingness to end debate. Supporters of the legislation called upon the majority leader to propose a cloture vote, but Lott decided not to take any action that might split the Republican Caucus. With Lott choosing not to take the reins, the Democrats were forced to file for cloture on June 11, 1998. The cloture motion was defeated on a 43–56 vote as Republicans treated the vote as a test of their ability to set the agenda.

Debate on S. 1415 continued for a few more days until Majority Leader Lott finally decided to put the bill out of its misery. Declaring that "I don't see how we are going to conclude this just by moving along at the slow pace we have been moving along," Lott filed a cloture motion on June 17, 1998.[51] He also obtained unanimous consent that Senator Ted Stevens (R-Alaska), chair of the Budget Committee, be recognized to raise a Budget Act point of order if the cloture vote failed. Fourteen Republicans joined with all but two of the Democrats to vote for cloture, but the 57–42 vote margin was still three votes short of the 60 needed to end debate. Senator Ford joined with Senator Charles S. Robb (D-Va.) to vote against cloture. Following the vote, Senator Stevens raised a point of order that the bill be recommitted to the Commerce Committee because its spending provisions violated budget limits contained in section 312(f) of the Congressional Budget Act. A Democratic motion to waive the Budget Act was rejected on a 53–46 vote. The vote signalled the end of S. 1415.

"UP IN SMOKE": LESSONS FROM THE DEFEAT OF S. 1415

Shortly after the defeat of S. 1415, Speaker Gingrich issued a statement giving his verdict on the bill's unceremonious demise. "The Senate bill drowned in a sea of money," he declared in typical style.[52] Majority Leader Lott pursued a similar theme when he expressed hope that Democrats would work with Republicans to produce legislation that would tackle the problem of underage smoking "without again resorting to the big government, big tax, big spending bill that was defeated today."[53] Both statements were indictments of the bill's supporters. President Clinton, Senator McCain, and Senator Kerry first lost control of the way that the issue was framed, and then found that they could not control the legislative process. Drafting a more narrowly focused bill, greater efforts to counter the advertising and lobbying campaign of the tobacco industry, and persuading antismoking zealots to ditch amendments that toughened the bill would have left opponents isolated and probably unable to muster the votes to defeat a cloture motion. The developing Monica Lewinsky scandal caused part of the problem. The

White House became increasingly distracted by the scandal, and did not devote the resources necessary to keep the debate over S. 1415 "on message"
and put pressure on senators to stick with the bill. A lack of parliamentary
power caused further problems. McCain worked hard to produce a compromise bill, but lacked the authority to impose his will upon the chamber without the support of Majority Leader Lott. The bill's demise owed much to the
majority leader's control over the agenda.

A number of general lessons can be drawn from the defeat of the Universal Tobacco Settlement Act that should prove useful to students of politics
and practitioners. First, the importance of framing the issue in favorable terms
is difficult to underestimate. The lesson is the same one that observers of politics from Machiavelli onwards have given: Control the terms of debate—do
not let opponents blur or distort the message. Second, legislation with a
narrow focus stands a better chance of passing than legislation that tries to
do too much too quickly. The broader the scope of a bill the more likely opponents will be able to mobilize further opposition to the legislation and
challenge the terms of debate. Third, the involvement of the White House
is a great aid to countering the centrifugal forces at work in Congress. A
president can help mobilize public opinion, define alternatives, and "lean"
upon waverers. Finally, passage of legislation is difficult to achieve without
the support of the majority leader. The majority leader is the only person
in the Senate with the parliamentary authority to bring a semblance of order
to proceedings.

NOTES

1. Quoted in Alan Greenblatt, "Tobacco Foes Look for Support," *Congressional Quarterly Week-ly Report*, 2 May 1998: 1154.
2. Quoted in Saundra Torry, "Far-Reaching Tobacco Bill Moves to Center Stage; Push for Change, Desire for New Revenue Propel Legislation and Senate Debate," *Washington Post*, 18 May 1998, A1.
3. Ibid.
4. The term "unbounded" is used by John Dryzek to describe an issue that is not easily con-tainable within a discrete policy arena. See John S. Dryzek, *Discursive Democracy* (Cambridge UK: Cambridge University Press, 1990).
5. *Congressional Record*, 105th Cong., 1st sess., 7 November 1997: S11997.
6. Good accounts of the events leading to the Tobacco Settlement of June 1997 are Peter Pringle *Cornered: Big Tobacco at the Bar of Justice* (New York: Henry Holt, 1998), and Carrick Mol-lenkamp, Adam Levy, Joseph Menn, and Jeffrey Rothfeder, *The People vs. Big Tobacco* (Prince-ton, NJ: Bloomberg Press, 1998).
7. Quoted in John F. Harris and Helen Dewar, "The Politics: White House, Hill Wary of Proposed Agreement," *Washington Post*, 21 June 1997, A1.
8. Testimony before the U.S. Senate, Committee on Commerce, Science, and Transportation, "The Global Settlement of Tobacco Litigation and Public Health," *Hearing*, 105th Congress, 2nd Sess., October 9, 1997.
9. The White House, Office of the Press Secretary, "Remarks by President Clinton and President Chirac in Photo Opportunity," June 20, 1997.

10. The White House, Office of the Press Secretary, "Remarks by the President on Tobacco Settlement Review," September 17, 1997.
11. See Noriko Hirabayashi "President Clinton's Strategies for Communications in the 1998 Tobacco Debate," *Japanese Journal of American Studies* 10 (1999): 112–113.
12. *Congressional Record*, 105th Cong., 1st sess., 7 November 1997: S11997.
13. Senator Orrin Hatch (R-Utah) gave evidence on two separate occasions.
14. Quoted in "McCain Delays Action on Tobacco Bill," *Washington Post*, 28 March 1998, A1.
15. The White House, Office of the Vice President, "Remarks on Anti-Smoking Legislation," February 11, 1998.
16. Ibid.
17. Quoted in Ceci Connolly and John Mintz, "For Cigarette Industry, a Future without GOP Support," *Washington Post*, 29 March 1998, A1.
18. The material in this paragraph is taken from James Carney, "Harsh Words, Strewn Chairs and Tobacco's Lost GOP Friends Mark a Difficult Negotiation," *Time*, 12 April 1998.
19. Quoted in John Schwartz, "Tobacco Firms Say They'd Rather Fight; RJR Chief Desires Legislative Plan as 'Punishment,'" *Washington Post*, 9 April 1998, A1.
20. The White House, Office of the Vice President, "Statement by Vice President Gore on R.J. Reynolds Tobacco Announcement," April 8, 1998.
21. Ibid.
22. Ibid.
23. Ibid.
24. Quoted in Saundra Torry, "Squabbles Go on over Tobacco Bill Changes," *Washington Post*, 6 June 1998, A4.
25. Quoted in Alan Greenblatt, "Tobacco Legislation's Rapid Pace Emboldens Backers, Confounds Foes," *Congressional Quarterly Weekly Report*, 16 May 1998: 1307.
26. *Congressional Record*, 105th Cong., 2nd sess., 13 May 1998: S4817.
27. Ibid.
28. Quoted in Ruth Marcus, "Big Tobacco Quietly Tries to Grow Grass Roots; Industry's Sophisticated Lobbying Tactics Strike Some Critics as Deceptive," *Washington Post*, 16 May 1998, A1.
29. *Congressional Record*, 105th Cong., 2nd sess., 18 May 1998: S5001.
30. Ibid.
31. Ibid.
32. Ibid., S5003.
33. Ibid., S5004.
34. Ibid., S5003.
35. Alexis Simendinger, "A Strategy, of Sorts, on Tobacco," *National Journal*, 14 February 1998: 350.
36. Saundra Torry and Helen Dewar, "Big Tobacco's Ad Blitz Felt in Senate Debate," *Washington Post*, 17 June 1998, A1.
37. Public Citizen, "Blowing Smoke: Big Tobacco's 1998 Congressional Lobbying Expenses Skyrocket," downloaded from <www.citizen.org/tobacco/oct98lobby.htm>.
38. Quoted in Howard Kurtz, "Attack Ads Carpet TV: High Road Swept Away; Distortions Rule the Airwaves," *Washington Post*, 20 October 1998, A1.
39. Quoted in Public Citizen "Burning Down the Houses," downloaded from <www.citizen.org/congress/covjus/tobacco/burning.htm>.
40. Quoted in Ceci Connolly, "GOP's Tack on Tobacco: A Fight against Taxes; Leaders Warn of Hazards of Regulation," *Washington Post*, 27 April 1998, A1.
41. Quoted in Alan Greenblatt, "Amendments and Ads Bury 'Inviolable' Tobacco Bill," *Congressional Quarterly Weekly Report*, 20 June 1998: 1669.
42. Quoted in Peter Baker and Saundra Torry, "Clinton Scolds Tobacco Lobby for Ad Campaign," *Washington Post*, 16 June 1998, A1.
43. The White House, Office of the Press Secretary, "Remarks by the President on Tobacco Legislation," 20 May 1998.
44. *Congressional Record*, 105th Cong., 2nd sess., 18 May 1998: S5006.
45. *Congressional Record*, 105th Cong., 2nd sess., 20 May 1998: S5151.
46. Quoted in Alan Greenblatt, "Tobacco Foes Hope Loaded Bill Will Be Hard to Say 'No' to," *Congressional Quarterly Weekly Report*, 6 June 1998: 1526.
47. *Congressional Record*, 105th Cong., 2nd sess., 9 June 1998: S5768.

48. Quoted in Mary Agnes Carey, "Anti-Drug Provisions Added," *Congressional Quarterly Weekly Report*, 13 June 1998: 1606.
49. Ibid., p. 1607.
50. Quoted in Alan Greenblatt, "Tobacco Foes Hope Loaded Bill Will Be Hard to Say 'No' to," 1527.
51. *Congressional Record*, 105th Cong., 2nd sess., 17 June 1998: S6473.
52. Quoted in Carter Eskew, "The Democrat Who Switched and Fought; Former Gore Confidant Formulated Tobacco Industry's Effective Ad Blitz," *Washington Post*, 19 June 1998, A1.
53. Ibid.

6

THE BATTLE OVER THE CENSUS

SEEKING TO INSTITUTIONALIZE
A PARTISAN ELECTORAL ADVANTAGE

THOMAS L. BRUNELL

The battle over the conduct of the census has been one of the fiercest fights on Capitol Hill in the past few years. Constitutionally mandated, the census is done every ten years by the Commerce Department's Bureau of the Census for the purpose of apportionment: allocating the number of members in the House of Representatives to each state.[1] Since the founding, however, at least two other important political functions of the census have emerged: the disbursement of billions of dollars in federal funding and the redistricting of state and federal legislative districts.

But probably one of the most important political functions to emerge from the decennial census, as it pertains to the institution of Congress, is redistricting, or political cartography as practitioners call it, which forces the nation's political system to constantly adjust for shifts in the demographics of population. For example, population estimates issued periodically by the Bureau indicate that the nation's population increased by nearly 11 percent or more than 27 million since 1990.[2] Once the population figures from the decennial census are gathered, apportionment is derived by a mathematical formula called the *Method of Equal Proportions*, a method used since the 1940s.[3] The idea is that proportional differences in the number of persons per representative for any pair of states should be kept to a minimum. The first fifty House seats are guaranteed by the Constitution: at least one representative per state. The question then becomes which state deserves more than one seat. As the nation's population shifts, states gain or lose congressional representation because the country's population keeps growing and the number of House seats remains at 435. Once congressional seats are apportioned, those states with more than one seat must create districts, with each district represented by a single member.

Because congressional seats are political prizes, census taking for the purposes of districting can be an instrument of partisan warfare. Following demographic and political trends for the 2000 census, California, Colorado, Nevada, and North Carolina add a member to their congressional delegations. Arizona, Florida, Georgia, and Texas each add two. On the other side of the ledger, Connecticut, Illinois, Indiana, Michigan, Mississippi, Ohio, Oklahoma, and Wisconsin lose a congressional seat, while New York and Pennsylvania drop two. Such state-by-state totals confirm a gain or loss in a state's power in the nation's capital.

The decennial census is an "actual enumeration," but two factors make taking the census a daunting task. The first is locating the legal residence of every individual who lives in the United States. Where, for example, do the homeless or other transients live? The second is getting those individuals to participate in the census by completing the survey that the Commerce Department sends to them. Both facets of the census routinely suffer from shortcomings. Census workers can make numerous errors, and individuals can refuse to cooperate. As a consequence, millions of Americans are routinely missed or ignored; others, such as college students living away from home, might be counted more than once;[4] and some, such as immigrants, especially migrant workers, can be counted in the wrong location. In 1990 alone there were roughly 26 million errors: About 10 million people were missed, 6 million people were counted twice, and 10 million were counted in the wrong place.[5]

Although the routine undercount of U.S. residents is a serious problem in and of itself, the fact that the individuals the census routinely misses are not distributed randomly across states, races, ethnic groups, and ages exacerbates the situation tremendously. The "differential undercount," as it is called, can undercount blacks, Hispanics, legal and illegal aliens, and urban residents. The Census Bureau has tried to alleviate this problem by proposing to significantly alter its census-taking methodology by using statistical sampling and survey techniques to evaluate the results of the census and subsequently adjust the population totals.[6]

Because population figures determine seats in the House of Representatives, set federal funding levels, and affect power in other indirect ways, both political parties have the potential to extract large political gains through the census process. Given the narrow majority in the House, for example, even the slightest shift in seats could mean reapportionment and thus the difference between majority and minority party status.

Democrats and Republicans fought fiercely over whether to adjust population totals using statistical sampling, a technique that scientifically estimates population in areas where traditional head-counting methods do not yield an accurate tally. Democrats supported sampling and adjusting the totals to catch certain hard-to-contact groups who tend to be Democrats, while many Republicans opposed such a method, asserting that it was illegal and would subject the census to political manipulation. Everyone, however, was equally concerned with the allocation of federal funds and reapportionment. And both sides of the partisan divide had the potential to extract large political gains through the redistricting process. It was not surprising therefore when Democrats and Republicans on Capitol Hill went to war over the 2000 Census, because even a relatively small shift in seats could mean the difference between majority and minority party status.

The skirmish, strategy, and acrimony between the Democratic and Republican parties over the census during the 105th and 106th Congresses (1997–1999 and 1999–2001) were near monumental. Both sides of the aisle fought intensely to advance and protect their political interests. The committee rooms, floor chambers, and hallways of Congress, the editorial pages of newspapers, and the hallowed chamber of the Supreme Court were all sites of this major partisan battle.

THE OPPOSING ARMIES AND THEIR STRATEGIES

Shortly after their historic takeover in 1995, House Republicans hastily sought to cut government and to marginalize certain special interests by eliminating three committees that were closely linked to Democratic allies: the District of Columbia Committee, Merchant Marine and Fisheries Committees, and the Post Office and Civil Service Committees. The Post Office and Civil Service Committee, which held jurisdiction over the census issue, maintained a subcommittee dedicated to oversight of the census. Originally, Republican leaders sought to do away with four standing committees and radically alter the jurisdiction of others. Fashioned for the most part from a plan by Representative David Dreier (R-Calif.) in his capacity as vice chairman of the Joint Committee on the Organization of Congress in the 103rd Congress (1993–1995), this plan met with strong resistance from some of the affected members when jurisdiction over the census was shifted to the Government Reform and Oversight Committee, originally chaired by Representative Bill Zeliff (R-N.H.) and later by Representative Dan Burton (R-Ind.).

THE REPUBLICAN BRASS

The GOP battle over the census was spearheaded in part from Speaker Newt Gingrich's (R-Ga.) "Dinosaur Room" in the Capitol building. A self-proclaimed "transformational figure," in less than six years Gingrich moved from being a backbencher despised by Democratic House leaders and mistrusted by members of his own party, to Speaker of the House of Representatives when the new Republican majority started in 1995.[7] Initially considered an oddity, when as an assistant professor of history at West Georgia College he ran as a Republican who favored civil rights and was fascinated by space travel and science fiction, Gingrich was for years Georgia's lone Republican representative in Congress. His career in politics, he said, dated from a visit to the ossuary at Verdun, France, where the sight of the bones of thousands of soldiers convinced him that politics matter.[8] Gingrich clearly understood the implications of an adjusted census and brought the resources of the majority party in Congress to bear in an attempt to halt the plan. Although the issue was difficult to manage given the complexity of statistical adjustment, the Speaker felt that it threatened the GOP majority in the House, a fact that made this issue central to the strength of his party.

Gingrich worked closely with Representative Dan Miller (R-Fla.), a smart and forceful conservative from Florida's 13th district who chaired the Subcommittee on the Census. A mild-mannered Ph.D. economist who taught statistics before going to Congress, Miller was a huge asset to the GOP as it fought the Democrats and the Clinton administration on using statistical sampling, mincing no words in making the case against sampling. "Statistics can be manipulated in a variety of ways," he argued.[9] Miller also strongly opposed President Clinton's nominee Ken Prewitt, director of the Census Bureau. "When I became chairman of the new Subcommittee on the Census," he declared on the House floor, "I made a controversial statement. I said I did not have any litmus test for the new census director. I said what we needed was a competent manager who was committed to working cooperatively with Congress." Miller went on to say:

> Unfortunately, I think the President had a litmus test. Dr. Prewitt's background does not have anything to suggest he can lead a huge organization at a time of crisis. He has admitted that he has never run anything of the magnitude of the Census Bureau. Basically, for a short time he ran a think tank, and that is it. The decennial census is the largest peacetime mobilization in American history. The Census Bureau needs a General Schwarzkopf, not a professor Sherman Klunk, to save the census. So why would the President nominate an academic? Because of politics. Dr. Prewitt supports the President's sampling scheme, so he received the nomination.[10]

Representative Miller's work on the topic brought him closer to another Republican who delved into the sampling issue—Representative J. Dennis Hastert (R-Ill.). Then-Deputy Majority Whip and now the House Speaker, Hastert led the GOP in the battle over the census. Before becoming Speaker at the beginning of the 106th Congress (1999–2001), Hastert sat on the Census Subcommittee, an assignment he agreed to largely to block Representative Chris Shays (R-Conn.), a moderate Republican who openly supported statistical adjustments to the census, from gaining a seat on the subcommittee. Affectionately called "The Coach" by his supporters because of his background as a high school wrestling coach, Hastert combined tenacity and congeniality to bring warring factions to the table to discuss compromise. This interest in passing legislation, even if it took Democratic votes, occasionally put him at odds with some activist conservatives in the GOP.[11]

The GOP leadership coordinated part of its attack with Representative Harold Rogers (R-Ky.), chair of the House Appropriations subcommittee that funds the departments of Commerce, Justice, and State. As chair of this subcommittee, Rogers subsequently oversaw spending bills used as vehicles for eliminating the Commerce Department and changing the way the decennial census would be conducted. An old-style *pol*, Rogers was known on the Hill for straying from various zealot party factions, especially when it concerned budget slashing. This fiscal conservatism was largely due to the fact that his Fifth Congressional District is one of the poorest districts of Kentucky, with many residents struggling to adapt to the long-term decline in coal mining and tobacco farming.[12]

Republican Hill leaders worried that the Clinton administration could abuse statistical sampling to boost the count in areas likely to vote Democratic, thereby threatening the fate of their already razor-thin majority. It was "a dagger aimed at the heart of our majority," claimed former Speaker Gingrich.[13] The GOP, therefore, used a multipronged approach in their attempt to block the use of statistical sampling in the census. First, they exercised their control over the House to pass legislation that blocked the use of sampling. Second, they filed two lawsuits in an attempt to get the courts to block the use of statistical sampling, questioning the constitutionality of sampling. Finally, they used the media and public hearings in their oversight capacity to make the case for an unadjusted census.

THE DEMOCRATIC BRASS

From the White House, President Bill Clinton remained fully committed to including sampling within the decennial census, always vetoing or threatening to veto any Republican legislation that sought to limit the Census Bureau's ability to fix the census. Vice President Al Gore was equally committed to holding the party line.

Liberal Representative Carolyn B. Maloney (D-N.Y.), who represents New York's 14th Congressional District, which irregularly includes parts of Manhattan, Queens, and Long Island, was given primary responsibility on the newly created subcommittee, charged with overseeing the census, for making the case that the GOP was playing politics with the 2000 census. The native North Carolinian accused the Republicans of refusing to authorize statistical sampling in the census because it would compensate for an undercount of minorities, who usually vote Democratic.[14] To prohibit sampling was "utterly irresponsible and devoid of moral imperative," she argued.[15] When the GOP leadership proposed establishing the special subcommittee panel of the Government Reform and Oversight Committee to consider the census issue, for example, Maloney balked. "This new subcommittee is the latest effort by the leadership," she said, "to politicize the census and make sure that millions of minorities and poor are left out of the count."[16]

As the top Democrat on the House Committee on Government Reform, Representative Henry A. Waxman (D-Calif.) contributed greatly to the Democrat's census campaign, bitterly fighting tooth and nail to blockade any Republican attempts to change the plan for the census. A significant player on Capitol Hill for nearly twenty years, Waxman represents the Golden state's 29th Congressional District, home to Hollywood and its movie lots. But this is where the Hollywood glitz ends; Waxman has never attended the Oscars ceremony. Rather, the California lawmaker has been described as a shrewd political operator who is a skilled and idealistic policy entrepreneur.[17] He was elected to Congress with the Class of 1974, the so-called "Watergate babies," after serving in the California State Assembly where he chaired the redistricting committee.

As someone representing a growing number of Haitian refugees, former Representative Carrie P. Meek (D-Fla.) of Florida's 17th Congressional District was no stranger to how the census can count immigrants in the wrong place, and was a vocal proponent of statistical sampling to alleviate the problems associated with counting minorities in the census. The granddaughter of a slave, she previously served in the state senate for a decade where she helped to draw the black majority district she would eventually serve.[18] Never backing down from a fight, Meek was well-known for instigating skirmishes with the other side of the aisle. In the 104th Congress (1995–1997), for example her House floor words scolding Speaker Gingrich's book deal with HarperCollins, speculated to be in the millions of dollars, were stricken from the *Congressional Record* because they were considered a personal attack on Gingrich. On another occasion, in the 105th Congress (1997–1999), Meek joined a group of House Democratic women who marched unannounced into Gingrich's office to demand that he call off an investigation of alleged voting irregularities in the 1996 California House election won by Democrat Lorretta Sanchez.[19]

Representing West Virginia's 1st Congressional District, Alan B. Mollohan, the son of a congressman, was the ranking minority member of the Commerce, Justice, State, and Judiciary Appropriations Subcommittee. A moderately liberal Democrat who normally concentrates on bringing projects to the district, Mollohan was a leader in the Democratic effort to permit the Census Bureau to prepare for the census with the aid of statistical sampling, characterizing the debate as a "horse and buggy versus modern transportation" argument.[20]

Using a different approach from their Republican counterparts, the Democrats framed the census battle as a civil rights fight.[21] They viewed statistical sampling as a way to increase their numbers in the House. Nevertheless, their message focused on the differential undercount and the fact that the inner-city, poor, non-English speakers and people living in remote areas would be missed at much higher rates than whites. Their rhetoric charged that the undercount undermines the principle of "one person, one vote" and costs the underrepresented areas millions of dollars in federal funding each year.[22]

THE INFANTRY STAFF

The majority staff of the Subcommittee on the Census was relatively large, having eleven full-time employees (a staff director, deputy staff director, staff counsel, two press aides, three investigators, two data/statistical staffers, and one clerk),[23] as opposed to the minority staff, which had just three full time aides. As with any congressional office, a slew of interns— most of whom stay for roughly two to three months—supplemented staff work. This inequity of staff was indicative of the importance the Republican leadership ascribed to the census issue. It also highlights how the majority party uses its control of congressional resources to put the minority party at a disadvantage. While such discrepancies may seem trivial to the general public, on Capitol Hill, a not-so-secret secret is that members of Congress rarely write anything for themselves. Congressional staff pen everything from constituent mail, *Dear Colleague* memos, letters to newspaper editors and full editorials, floor speeches, and questions and remarks for committee witnesses.

The relationship between a subcommittee chairman and the subcommittee staff was fairly close, although a degree of independence was apparent on occasion.[24] Staff were in daily contact with Representative Miller's personal office who would meet either directly with the representative himself or with his chief of staff or legislative director. These meetings were designed to coordinate the day-to-day strategy of the subcommittee as well as the long-term strategy with the party leadership.

Much of what the subcommittee staff did revolved around public relations, with a premium on press coverage. Staffers for both sides kept regular score of which side received better coverage. When Democrats were getting better press coverage on the census issue, for example, Republican staffers would say "we are losing the battle." When the GOP had one or two positive stories in the press someone would declare, "the tide has turned." Every morning one of the staffers would use an on-line account to find all articles that even mentioned the "census." These daily "clips" are then distributed to all staff members each day to ensure that we are up-to-the-minute informed of press coverage. This is standard operating procedure on the Hill and our office was no exception. This in addition to the fact that the office received at least four daily papers, two weekly papers that covered the Hill exclusively, four different weekly news magazines, and seven television sets all tuned to C-SPAN. The hypersensitivity paid to press coverage struck me as irrational. Nonetheless, this sensitivity is real and it is indicative of the nature of the political game.

Both parties used the media to embarrass the other side or to expose perceived exaggerations. At one point in the census battle, Representative Maloney wrote a letter to the editor in the *Washington Post*, making a point about the census with reference to the thirteen original states, and later wrote about the other thirty-nine states—for a total of fifty-two. Republicans quickly and gleefully jumped all over this mistake, pointing out that perhaps Representative Maloney had used statistical sampling to arrive at fifty-two states in the union. Small "victories" like this one would significantly affect the morale of the staff for at least a day or two. The Democrats did not have a monopoly on these gaffes. At one point after the Supreme Court decision, which stated that statistical sampling was not allowed by law for the purposes of apportionment, the Republican staff sought to hold a hearing entitled "Statistical Sampling Ruled Illegal." The statisticians at the Census Bureau found this oversimplified statement amusing.[25] The investigative staff was broadly charged with keeping tabs on what the Bureau was doing in preparation for the upcoming census, as well as handling outreach to interested parties, of which there are many. From hearings, to press conferences, to meetings of the numerous advisory boards to the Census Bureau, there were enough public events at which we were "needed" to keep most of the staff quite busy.

THE BUREAUCRATS

Ken Prewitt, director of the Bureau of the Census, was chosen in 1998 by President Clinton to head the Census Bureau. Having earned his doctorate in political science from Stanford, Prewitt came to Capitol Hill by way of a long career in academia, first as president of the Social Science Research Council, then as director of the University of Chicago's National Opinion Research Corporation, and finally as chair of the University of Chicago's Department of Political Science. Prewitt was appointed as director in the midst of the battle over the sampling issue and consistently defended the "new" census. Howard R. Hogan, director of the Decennial Statistical Studies Section, was the Bureau's point man. Mild mannered and extremely proficient in the uses of statistics for adjusting the census, Hogan was responsible for explaining and defending the statistical procedures to be used. And then there was John H. Thompson, the associate director for the Decennial Census. Thompson joined Hogan as one of two people who regularly met with congressional staff to discuss census proposals. No stranger to the heated battle over adjusting the census (he was deeply involved in the 1990 skirmish), Thompson brought both a statistical background and a deep-rooted knowledge of how the census works to the table. Never without a Tootsie Roll Pop dangling from his mouth, he was extremely congenial in the face of heated passions over the topic, calmly discussed the merits of adjusting the census with modern scientific methods, and was ready to deliver a history lesson on the census at any time.

THE BATTLE BEGINS

In one of the earliest confrontations over the census, Republican leaders tried to manipulate the legislative process to ban the use of statistical sampling in the census. In a procedural move reminiscent of the kinds of political machinations used by the leaders of the majority party in both chambers, the GOP House leadership attached a rider prohibiting statistical sampling amendment to a bill that contained provisions for flood relief. This took place in June 1997, shortly after massive floods affected thirty-five states. Undaunted by the potential for bad publicity and the reality of denying aid to people whose lives were uprooted by the flood, the president vetoed a spending bill that included $5.4 billion for disaster aid to flood victims because of the statistical sampling amendment and another politically inspired rider that was designed to prevent a government shutdown in the event of a budget impasse, such as the two that proved so harmful to the GOP in the winter of 1995.[26]

President Clinton's rapid veto reflected his view that the politics of this potentially high-stakes dispute were on his side, just as they were when polls showed the public held Republicans more accountable for two partial government shutdowns. Clinton and the Democrats held their ground and the Republicans temporarily retreated. The GOP leadership was promptly hounded in the press for its failed political attempt to control the census. The Democrats appeared to win the first battle in what would become a three-year war over the census.

CONGRESSIONAL HEARINGS

One of Congress's most important functions is executive branch oversight. The intent of these legislative workshops is often seen in three alternative perspectives: to arrive at the common good of the larger society, to further the interest of individual legislators, and to grapple with complexity. The truth of these conceptual portraits has varied over time and across committees. Some hearings take on features of a legislative court where members decide what to do based upon the evidence of law and fact brought before them by the interested parties. They furnish information with which members can educate themselves on the issues involved in a bill, and they serve as a clearinghouse for information needed by all the contestants in the legislative process.[27] The Census Subcommittee held numerous hearings on the census to focus attention on the issue and to build a case for specific legislation. These meetings witnessed a struggle between competing groups, none of whom were concerned with a guiding abstraction like the common good. Committee members acted as advocates of their partisan clientele and not as neutral judges seeking the general good. Census hearings therefore were not neutral fact-finding tribunals but vehicles to advance the interests of committee members. At times they allowed for the transmission of information from the various interest groups to the committee. On other occasions they were used as a propaganda platform by the committee members, with little thought given to a meaningful debate.

Republicans single-handedly decided on the time, location, and specific subject matter. While Democratic members invited token witnesses, the majority restricted these to far fewer than their own experts, a tactic designed to garner favorable press coverage and score points publicly against the other party. The "Oversight of the 2000 Census: Serious Problems with Statistical Adjustment Remain" hearing on the validity of the statistical model planned for use to adjust the official census population totals highlighted Republican's unilateral control over the proceedings. A number of sympathetic academics were invited as experts, with the intent of testifying to all of the problems—statistically and operationally—of the Democratic statistical sampling plan. Democrats invited three witnesses who took the opposing view that sampling would fix many of the inaccuracies of the census.

Trying to exploit the problems associated with the sampling plan was just one aspect of the overall Republican strategy. Staff organized official hearings and unofficial meetings with the Census Bureau to learn about the issues involved and to receive updates on various aspects of the sampling plan. Some of the topics covered besides the statistical sampling plan included a paid advertising program, dress rehearsals by the Bureau, and community outreach programs. Working relationships also were formed with a small segment of the academic community who were familiar with statistical sampling and the census and whose research demonstrated the problems with sampling. This facilitated rapport and mutual confidence.

Preparing for hearings can be an intense process, and the September 17 hearing on the census was no exception. Witnesses submitted their written testimonies forty-eight hours in advance of the hearing to enable staff to prepare questions for both "friendly" and "unfriendly" witnesses. This would allow for committee members to purposely elicit targeted responses from witnesses. Despite some knowledge by members, staff from both parties coached their bosses on a play-by-play basis.

Chairman Miller convened the hearing with an opening statement, followed by Representative Maloney, the ranking Democratic member. Both members used the opportunity to restate their party's position on sampling in the Census. Miller cautioned that sampling was risky and would imperil the Census Bureau's ability to deliver the census data accurately and on time. Maloney reiterated the Democratic position supporting sampling and the importance of including an accurate count of blacks, Hispanics, American Indians, and others who are typically missed in the census.

Following opening remarks the subcommittee heard testimony from the first panel of witnesses.[28] In typical fashion, each expert was limited to approximately five minutes, followed by five minutes of questioning by each subcommittee member. The partisanship of the process rang loud and clear.

Republicans asked hard probing questions of Democratic witnesses and lobbed softballs to their own witnesses. Similarly, Democrats made their own witnesses look good and discredited those witnesses appearing at the request of Republicans.

FLOOR DEBATE

The census issue was debated on the House floor in connection with a number of pieces of legislation, including appropriations for the Census Bureau. The single most partisan and contentious debate took place during the appropriations process. Although the appropriations bill included full funding for the Departments of Commerce, Justice, and State, a "fence" was erected around the funding for the Census Bureau that only released six months worth of funding, thus requiring additional congressional action for the release of other monies. The measure provided the GOP another chance to affect the outcome of how the census should be conducted. The debate did not revolve around this technicality, but rather the merits of the use of sampling.

The rules governing the debate allowed Democrats to offer one amendment consisting of substitute language supporting statistical sampling in the census, and allowed for two hours of debate. Representative Alan B. Mollohan, a Democrat from West Virginia's 1st Congressional District, who introduced the amendment, controlled sixty minutes. The other hour was controlled by Representative Rogers.

Each floor manager spoke briefly before yielding time to their colleagues to speak about the census issue. Each side then used speeches and visual aids to make their points, with Democrats stressing the undercount and its inherent unfairness toward minorities, and Republicans arguing that the program was problematic and untested. The most poignant case for Democrats came from Representative Meek:

> There are a lot of things in this census that you [the Republicans] are not even thinking about. The Voting Rights Act is in there. My people died for the right to vote. If you are going to skew the figures because you do not want to count them correctly, that removes the humor from this situation for me. For the past six censuses you have undercounted African-Americans. It is time to tell this country we want everybody counted. I have been working on this census issue since the 104th Congress. Now the time for this gag is over. You may as well cut it [sampling] out, because we are going to let the American public know that you are taking the right that the Constitution gave us, enumeration. Define it for me. I have never seen it defined in the Constitution. It does not say that you count every head, that that is enumeration. Enumeration could include sampling. You cannot prove to me through any kind of empirical observation that it means what you are saying it means.[29]

Representative James Traficant (D-Ohio), who eventually defected from his party, gave a short speech extolling the virtues of the Constitution and the traditional method of census taking:

> Let me warn the Democrats, sampling is an axe that can cut both ways. Those in fact who support it one day may oppose it another. Those who may benefit one day may get ripped off the other day. I just want to close out by saying Congress should confine itself to some basic parameters, which include following the Constitution. We were elected and we took an oath to uphold the Constitution, not the charter of the United Nations or some scientific methodology by a group of scientists who, in fact, are not aligned with mainstream America in just their matters of theology. The world was once flat, all the scientists told us that. My community, they say, will be hurt without sampling. My community will be hurt if we do not have an honest head count because, in the final analysis, whoever is doing that sampling some day might not like the makeup of my district.[30]

The Republicans' case was best articulated by then-Deputy Majority Whip Hastert, who spoke about the Bureau's plan to sample for nonresponse follow-up, which would collect census data for only 90 percent of all households:

> The dirty little secret of this plan is that the poll, not actual enumeration, is their [the Census Bureau and, by implication, the Democrats] first priority. In short, under the Census scheme proposed by this administration, actually counting people is incidental to the final count—our population, and its characteristics, will be determined by polling guesstimates. Why did the Census Bureau decide that they needed to count 90 percent of the population? Mr. Chairman, it is my belief that this figure itself was chosen for political reasons—it was the smallest number they felt the Congress and the American people could swallow. The plan to count 90 percent is a fig leaf, a subterfuge, a sham designed to cover-up their population polling scheme. Make no mistake about it, the final numbers will be determined by a poll and they will not be dependent in any way, shape, or form upon actual enumeration. Furthermore, if for any reason the polling scheme fails, we are up the proverbial creek because the Census Bureau will have stopped counting at 90 percent.[31]

In an unusual show of force, Minority Leader Richard Gephardt (D-Mo.) and Speaker Gingrich each joined their party ranks on the floor to support their respective positions. "The census is today's great civil rights issue, and once again they are standing against what is right," Gephardt declared.[32] "That transfers to politicians an amount of power that none of the Founding Fathers would have ever agreed to," responded Gingrich. "Don't ask the people of the United States to rely on politicians to control pollsters to count virtual citizens."[33]

Despite impassioned pleas by Democrats, Republicans held their troops tightly together to defeat the Mollohan amendment 227 to 201.[34] Only seven members deserted party lines. Five Democrats voted against the proposal: Leonard L. Boswell of Iowa, Gene Taylor of Mississippi, James A. Traficant, Jr. of Ohio, Virgil H. Goode, Jr. of Virginia and Ralph M. Hall of Texas. Just two Republicans voted for the proposal: Chris Shays of Connecticut and Constance A. Morella of Maryland. None of the crossover votes were particularly surprising in that these members are all known as political moderates.

THE COURT ENTERS THE FRAY

In the 1998 appropriations for the Departments of Commerce, Justice, and State the parties agreed to have expedited review of lawsuits regarding the use of sampling in the census. Section 209(e)(2), 111 Stat. 2482 states: "It shall be the duty of a U.S. district court hearing an action brought under this section and the Supreme Court of the United States to advance on the docket and to expedite to the greatest possible extent the disposition of any such matter." The compromise between the parties was that the Census Bureau would be allowed to go ahead with the sampling plan in their dress rehearsals, to be held in Sacramento, California, Columbia, South Carolina, and on an Indian reservation in Menomonie, Wisconsin. Republicans were also allowed to use governmental funds in their lawsuit against the Bureau.[35]

The GOP took its case against sampling to the U.S. Supreme Court in January 1999. *U.S. House of Representatives v. Department of Commerce* marked the first time that the House of Representatives, as an institution, filed a lawsuit. The judiciary was called on to settle as a matter of statutory interpretation the controversy over the Census Bureau's proposed use of statistical samples and adjustments in conducting the 2000 census. The lower court that heard the case ruled unanimously that the law prohibited the use of sampling in the census. Justices noted in part that the use of statistical sampling to determine the population for purposes of apportioning representatives in Congress among the states violated the Census Act. In another lawsuit filed by the Southeastern Legal Foundation, a conservative public interest law firm, Matt Glavin, the president of the foundation said: "Our intent has been simple and clear from the beginning. We will challenge the use of sampling for apportioning Congress as unconstitutional because the law is clear: no sampling as a substitute for an 'actual enumeration.'"[36] While the arguments about the two cases overlapped considerably there were some key distinctions, notably that the parties involved in the two cases differed; in one case it was the members of the House of Representatives and in the other case it was a series of private individuals.

ORAL ARGUMENTS

Nearly the entire staff of the Census Subcommittee, as well as numerous members of Congress, and high-ranking Census employees were present for the oral arguments when *U.S. House of Representatives v. Department of Commerce* reached the Supreme Court. Because the case enjoined two cases, the normal court allotment of an hour—thirty minutes for each side to argue their case—was increased to an hour and a half by the High Bench, with each side allocated forty-five minutes.

Solicitor General Seth Waxman represented the position of the Clinton administration. He focused on the fact that the census has historically had a tough time enumerating the population and statistical sampling could help alleviate some of these mistakes. The nine justices focused on factual questions such as what the Census Bureau explicitly planned in terms of using sampling in the census. At one point Chief Justice Rehnquist asked how the Census Bureau knew it missed people if the census itself was supposed to be the accurate measure of the population. Waxman responded by noting that the answer was through demographic analysis, which uses birth and death records that give a relatively accurate picture of the national population in the country. Justice Scalia then asked Waxman his interpretation of the phrase, to which the solicitor general responded with an analogy to counting the number of people in Camden Yards during an Orioles game. Scalia followed up with a question as to whether or not this fit the criterion as an actual enumeration. The sparring over language continued for a number of minutes as to why the adjective "actual" should be inserted. Waxman argued that since the constitution divvied up the seats in the House presumably based on estimates, the founders wanted to ensure that in 1790 actual data were tabulated to reapportion as soon as possible. The position of the administration was that statistical sampling techniques were essentially unknown at the time of the founding and there is no reason constitutional or otherwise to prohibit the use of scientific methods to improve the census.

Lawyers for the Republicans were questioned at length, especially by Justice Scalia, as to whether a precedent existed for the Supreme Court to step in between the executive and legislative branches to resolve what was essentially a political dispute. Specifically, Scalia wanted citation to a case between the presidency and Congress. Republican lawyers noted *U.S. v. Nixon*, *INS v. Chadha*, and *Senate Select Committee v. Nixon*. "I don't like injecting us into a battle between the two political branches. I think they will survive. I am not sure we will," concluded Justice Scalia. Other justices suggested that if the House did not agree with the president on this issue they should not appropriate money for the White House, that is, a governmental shutdown at 1600 Pennsylvania Avenue. Questions then turned to reasonable methods of census taking. In response to one question regarding what a census taker should do if he or she was certain someone lived in a house but was unwilling to answer the door, Republican lawyers suggested that an appropriate action was to record zero people living at that address.

THE DECISION

On January 5, 1999, the Supreme Court released its ruling. The Supreme Court decided, much like the lower courts, that sampling was illegal based upon the current wording of the Census Act. It was not ruled unconstitutional vio a-vis the "actual enumeration" phrase in the constitution since the Court often prefers to answer a question on statutory grounds as opposed to constitutional grounds. This leaves a degree of uncertainty about how the justices actually felt about the constitutional phraseology.

Getting wind of the ruling early, the subcommittee dispatched three staffers up the street to retrieve a copy of the decision. After obtaining a copy of the decision, staff tried to digest what the justices had written. It quickly became evident that the ruling did not derail the plans for sampling altogether. While the Court's decision blocked one controversial aspect of the plan—Sampling for Nonresponse Follow-up (SNRFU)—it did leave the door open for the coverage evaluation survey. That is, by law the Census Bureau could not use statistical sampling in enumerating the population for the purposes of apportionment.[37] This meant that the Census Bureau would have to do a 100 percent nonresponse follow-up, thus sending an enumerator to each and every household that did not respond to the census by mail.

BACK ON THE HILL

The decision was a partial victory for both sides of the partisan divide: For Democrats the census would still conduct the follow-up survey with the figures adjusted for everything but apportionment; for Republicans, sampling was ruled illegal for apportionment purposes and the SNRFU portion of the plan was scrapped, meaning that a full set of unadjusted census data would be available. But Republicans kept looking for a way to reduce the likelihood that the census would or could be adjusted with the follow-up survey. To accomplish this they concentrated on what is called Post-Census Local Review (PCLR). PCLR concerns the provision that cities and other localities are provided with a grace period after the census for reviewing the data and noting any errors to the Bureau before the data are officially reported.

Republicans believed this would improve census accuracy, but PCLR also had the secondary effect of complicating the process. Given sufficient time and resources a review of the census data by localities would undoubtedly improve the count. Unfortunately, it made the job of delivering the numbers exponentially more difficult. For this reason the Bureau objected to the use of PCLR, noting it would delay the adjustment process and open the Bureau to potential lawsuits from thousands of localities.

BIPARTISAN NO-MAN'S LAND

A no-man's land existed between Democrats and Republicans and on some points of the census issue. In an apparent show of bipartisanship both sides of the aisle teamed up to write legislation making it possible for individuals on public assistance to have a temporary job with the Bureau and not risk losing any of their benefits. The political benefit of this proposal was to increase the number of enumerators working in the inner city who were familiar with the area and its residents. This, in turn, would increase the likelihood of accurately counting inner city residents who are among the highest levels of undercount in the decennial census. It is one part of a larger plan to facilitate "community-based enumeration."

In another effort to facilitate bipartisanship, subcommittee chair Dan Miller joined forces with Representative Meek to write the Decennial Census Improvement Act of 1999. With help from Legislative Counsel, a nonpartisan office available to staff and members responsible for turning ideas into legal legislation, the measure was relatively straightforward, exempting any money earned by temporary employees of the Census Bureau from affecting any other federal assistance programs, such as welfare and food stamps. Proponents of the legislation believed this would increase the pool of eligible people, especially in urban areas, who might work as enumerators in the 2000 Census. Like so many of the 10,000 or so bills introduced each congressional session, the measure would languish in the legislative process.

CONCLUSION

As of early 2003 the battles over the last census had ended. Indeed, after much political wrangling, and dozens of court cases across the country, the states redrew their congressional and state legislative district lines prior to the 2002 elections. In the end, all redistricting was done using the raw, unadjusted census data. There were significant problems with the statistical adjustment and the Census Bureau has not released the statistically adjusted population data. John Thompson, Associate Director of the Census Bureau, remarked of the adjusted data: "We were afraid it would be less accurate."[38] There were many positive aspects of the actual headcount in the most recent census; rather than being the most undercounted groups as they were in prior censuses, American Indians living on reservations were almost certainly over counted. Nonetheless, some racial groups were still systematically missed in the count. African Americans were clearly still undercounted and it is possible that the census had a net undercount for Hispanics and Asian Pacific Islanders. Interestingly, the most recent estimates indicate that there was a net over count of over 1.3 million people in the census—this in contrast with the initial report of a three million person undercount.[39]

The political skirmishes over the 2000 census involved the most powerful people in the nations' capital, including congressional leadership, the president, and the Supreme Court. After the ruling by the court both sides of the House agreed to a ceasefire when it became apparent that the census would move forward with the plan for a follow up survey. Indeed, in April 1999, Speaker Dennis Hastert (R-Ill.) sent a memo to Democratic Leader Richard Gephardt (R-Mo.) stating that the House had reached a stalemate with respect to 'legislative solutions' for the census, and that they [House members] should "move forward and let courts resolve the remaining issues."[40] But lawmakers and students of American politics understand that such a cessation of hostilities is temporary by definition. The fireworks will begin anew in the years running up to the next census in 2010. Self-interested members of Congress will always be keenly interested in the methods by which people are counted, given that their political livelihood depends on it.

NOTES

1. Article 1, Section 2 stipulates an actual enumeration be done every ten years.
2. Steven A. Holmes, "Census Data Is Due as Congress Braces for a Reshuffling," *Washington Post*, 27 December 2000, A1, A15.
3. This method is only one of several mathematical formulas that have been used. The major fractions method was used from 1911 to 1940, which yields slightly different results.
4. The Census Bureau counts people where they live for the majority of the year. Students, for example, are counted at their residence on campus rather than at home.
5. *Congressional Record*, 105th Cong., 1st sess., 26 February 1998: H650.
6. Thomas L. Brunell, "Redistricting in the 'Aughts': The Impact of a Two-Number Census," *American Review of Politics*, forthcoming; and Thomas L. Brunell, "Using Statistical Sampling to Estimate the U.S. Population: The Methodological and Political Debate over Census 2000." Typescript, 2000.
7. Michael Barone and Grant Ujifusa, *The Almanac of American Politics, 1998* (Washington, D.C.: National Journal, 1997), p. 420.
8. Ibid.
9. Quoted in Congressional Quarterly, Inc., *Politics in America 2000: The 106th Congress* (Washington, D.C.: Congressional Quarterly 1999), p. 322.
10. *Congressional Record*, 105th Cong., 1st sess., 23 June 1998: H5038.
11. Congressional Quarterly, Inc., *Politics in America 2000: The 106th Congress*, p. 458.
12. Congressional Quarterly, Inc., *Politics in America 2000: The 106th Congress*, p. 560.
13. Quoted in Steven A. Holmes, "Census Fight Is Put on Hold until a Count Is Completed," *New York Times*, 31 October 1999, A34.
14. Congressional Quarterly, Inc., *Politics in America 2000: The 106th Congress*, p. 943. Like Chairman Miller, Representative Maloney dedicates a portion of her homepage to the census issue: <http://www.house.gov/maloney/issues/census/index.html>.
15. Quoted in ibid., p. 943.
16. Quoted in ibid., p. 943.
17. Barone and Ujifusa, *The Almanac of American Politics, 1998*, p. 215.
18. Ibid., p. 382.
19. Congressional Quarterly, Inc., *Politics in America 2000: The 106th Congress*, p. 334.
20. Quoted in ibid., 1473.
21. John Mercurio, "Sampling Fight Continues, but Does It Really Matter?" *Roll Call*, 14 September 1998: 8.

22. The General Accounting Office (GAO) studied this topic at the request of the subcommittee. "Formula Grants: Effects of Adjusted Population Counts on Federal Funding to the States," February 1999, GAO/HEHS-99-69.
23. Tom Hofeller served as staff director for two years. He holds a Ph.D. in political science and is a redistricting expert. After his tenure at the subcommittee he moved to the Republican National Committee to serve as the director of redistricting for the upcoming round of district line drawing. Tom Brierton came to the subcommittee from Representative Hastert's office. He involved himself in the issue from its conception and played a large role in the hardball political aspects of the census issue. Jennifer Safavian was the counsel for the subcommittee. Previously she served as counsel for the Committee on Government Reform. George "Chip" Walker was the press secretary and Jo Powers served as assistant press secretary. Tim Maney, Erin Yeatman, and Lara Chamberlain comprised the investigative staff. David Flaherty was responsible for understanding the statistical plan and keeping in touch with the statistical community. Flaherty is a data expert who cut his teeth at the Republican National Committee's (RNC) computing center in the two previous presidential elections. Kelly Duquin clerked for the subcommittee. Like all Capitol Hill offices, the subcommittee's office had a platoon of interns, most of whom stayed for roughly two to three months.
24. This relationship undoubtedly varies from committee to committee depending on both the staff and the chairman.
25. Although both the Supreme Court and Congress have considerable power, neither can repeal the Law of Large Numbers.
26. John F. Harris and Helen Dewar, "President Vetoes Flood Relief Bill; Amendments on Shutdowns, Census Sampling Unresolved," *Washington Post*, 10 June 1997, A1.
27. Arthur Maass, *Congress and the Common Good* (New York: Basic Books, 1983).
28. There were a total of three panels at this hearing. The five majority witnesses were split into two panels and the three witnesses for the minority were on the last panel.
29. *Congressional Record*, 105th Cong., 1st sess., 5 August 1998: H7199.
30. *Congressional Record*, 105th Cong., 1st sess., 5 August 1998: H7208.
31. *Congressional Record*, 105th Cong., 1st sess., 5 August 1998: H7197.
32. Quoted in Juliet Eilperin, "House Rejects Full Census Funding, Setting up Clash with Clinton," *Washington Post*, 8 August 1998: A4.
33. Quoted in ibid.
34. For the full debate and recorded vote, see *Congressional Record*, 105th Cong., 1st sess., 5 August 1998: 7184–7212.
35. Editorial Desk, "Taking Leave of the Census," *New York Times*, 17 January 1998, A12.
36. Quoted in John Mercurio, "Statistics Skeptic Rep. Dan Miller Wins Chair of New Subcommittee on Census," *Roll Call*, 24 November 1997: 4.
37. In practice the Census Bureau still employs various aspects of statistical sampling for the purposes of apportionment. For instance, they will impute data, both partial demographic data and whole household data, if they are unable to enumerate a particular household.
38. Quoted in D'Vera Cohn, "Bureau Opposes Adjusting Census; Officials Say Count May Be More Precise," *Washington Post*, 2 March 2001, A1.
39. "Statement of Census Bureau Director C. Louis Kincannon on Accuracy and Coverage Evaluation Revision II," 14 March 2002, Washington, D.C., Department of Commerce.
40. Quoted in John Mercurio, "Census Battle Will be Fought in Courts Instead of Congress," *Roll Call*, 26 April 1999: 1.

7

LESSONS FROM THE BATTLEFIELD

COLTON C. CAMPBELL AND PAUL S. HERRNSON

When discussing how Congress works, one former lawmaker compared the institution to a large suburban high school. He said that there is a principal (the Speaker), teachers who run the classrooms (committee chairs), upperclassmen and women (senior members), and bells that tell people to go from class to class (or when to vote); the institution even has its own cafeteria and gymnasium. But most important, the tools that make someone popular and successful in high school also apply to Congress: a willingness to volunteer for tough yet tedious assignments, like canvassing colleagues to determine their positions on an upcoming vote (a whip count); a skill in reading and understanding people in order to disarm and coax them (lobbying); and a penchant for raising money to the betterment of the junior or senior class (to obtain reelection). Just as excellent performance in class, perfect attendance, and being well-groomed and courteous will likely get someone voted "the most likely to succeed" in his or her senior class, so, too, will those attributes get members noticed on Capitol Hill.[1]

Such comparisons are useful, but the metaphoric image of war more accurately illustrates contemporary congressional politics, perhaps because military and legislative battles are both struggles of opposing human wills, involving strategy, tactics, intelligence, and coordination.[2] One observer described the legislative rules as "the codes of battle," saying that the process can result in "a compromise, an armed truce, a prelude to the next conflict, or, more rarely, an all-out victory for one side."[3]

Of the different forms of political warfare that routinely unfold on Capitol Hill—skirmishes between committees over jurisdiction, conference fights between the House and Senate, clashes among factions, and attempted coups by young Turks to overthrow the Old Guard—the real conflict stems from the distinctly partisan alignment between Democrats and Republicans and their subsequent struggle for majority status. This is easy to forget because the Democrats maintained a dominant position in both chambers for much of the forty years preceding the Republican takeover. Congress was portrayed not as a battlefield where two partisan armies fought each other, but as a marketplace where 535 individual entrepreneurs bartered with one another.[4] Scholarly books on Congress contain many references to economists, but few to military strategists like Clausewitz or Sun Tzu.[5]

Life on Capitol Hill is now 180 degrees the opposite. In the past decade, both the Democrats and the Republicans have struggled to control the agenda on Capitol Hill and sought power through elections, yet both have wound up in near equal balance. Without working majorities the parties compile records geared to the next campaign cycle rather than negotiating legislative results.

There is little desire to cool partisan warfare as both sides position themselves for coming political battles. In the words of centrist Senator John Breaux (D-La.): "The parties have increasingly taken the position that it's my way or no way—so what we end up with is no way. . . . It's all about message."[6] During the Senate debate of the Patients' Bill of Rights legislation in the summer of 2001, for example, the two parties each set up opposing headquarters from which leadership directed deliberation and got out the word: Democrats naming their room the "ICU"—intensive communications unit—with Republicans calling their room the "delivery room," meaning delivery of a bill that, among other things, would be signed by the president.[7] Both rooms were decorated with all the technological gizmos needed to get out their respective messages, from computers for interactive chat to cameras and microphones for senators to use for interviews.

Despite the kisses, smiles, hugs, handshakes, and pledges that the past is over and a new day has dawned, lurking beneath and ready to explode are very real partisan disputes over policy specifics, personal tensions, power struggles, and the constant pressure-cooker atmosphere of a looming election that could turn the tide and change party control. Polarizing forces dominate the House as the two parties often battle in stalemate over legislative proposals reflecting their ideological differences. After the polarizing Clinton impeachment battle, the sky-high stakes of each election, and the razor-thin GOP majority in the House, battle lines have been drawn. Democrats and Republicans see to it that policy platforms are erected to please party constituents, agendas negotiated, campaign funds raised and doled out, nonincumbent challengers drafted and trained, floor leaders elected, committee assignments made, floor debates organized and scheduled, and winning coalitions built.[8] In this sense, parties strongly resemble modern armies that try to rouse their troops to subordinate their narrow self-interest and goals for the betterment of the whole.[9] House Minority Leader Richard Gephardt (D-Mo.) personified this when, in an unusual motivation tool for his rank and file, he showed clips from the Mel Gibson movie "Braveheart" to rouse his fellow Democrats for their fight over a Republican-sponsored bill on Medicare coverage for prescription drugs.[10] A few months later he went one step further, arriving at a Caucus session wearing a breastplate, tartan blanket, and face paint. "It's time to pick up the spears!" he roared.[11]

Even the Senate has become contentious, in spite of its "folkways"—the informal, member-to-member understandings about apprenticeship for newcomers, the elaborate courtesies, the institutional pride—that normally temper partisan fervor.[12] For years, senators (which in Latin means "old men") treasured their independence. Unlike their House counterparts, Senate party leaders traditionally have far fewer resources with which to promote party unity. The chamber's flexible rules provide only a skeletal framework for procedure, thereby enhancing the power of individual senators. Leading the Senate, reminisced Democratic Majority Leader Tom Daschle of South Dakota, was like "loading toads into a wheelbarrow." Even the physical structure of the chamber encourages individualism, with senators assigned particular seats. Together, these nonmajoritarian features generally insure individual senators greater independence, dilute partisanship, and generally limit party government. In a supposed anecdote about the Senate, Thomas Jefferson asks George Washington why he consented to the idea of a Senate. "Why did you pour that coffee into your saucer?" asks Washington. "To cool it," replies Jefferson. "Even so," replies Washington, "we pour legislation into the senatorial saucer to cool it."[13] For James Madison, that saucer would embody "enlightened citizens, whose limited number and firmness might reasonably interpose against impetuous councils."[14]

In contemporary times, senatorial decisions are still made with attention to historical precedent (established in a variety of written and unwritten ways), which the august body relies upon to clarify and preserve its legislative practices as well as to provide the road signs on the Senate's legislative map, but their decisions are increasingly crafted with partisan purpose. As Bailey demonstrates in his chapter, passing legislation in the contemporary Senate remains challenging. The sponsors of a bill would be wise to secure the support of congressional leaders, a large coalition of rank-and-file legislators, the administration, and an array of relevant interest groups. Gaining sympathetic treatment from the mass media can also go a long way in rallying public support, which has the potential to influence the votes of members of Congress.

Even traditionally nonpartisan positions, such as the Senate parliamentarian, the chamber's referee, have become victims of collateral damage. Sitting just below the presiding officer, or "president" of the Senate, and to his right, the parliamentarian has long been the quiet voice for the rule of law on the Senate floor who ensures that the game is fair. Presiding officers invariably follow the counsel of the parliamentarian on procedural questions and precedents; the parliamentarian also assists in the referral of legislation and other communications to the appropriate Senate committees. As a practical matter, the parliamentarian's rulings can be overturned only by a 60-vote majority, but that rarely happens. During debate, the acting president of the Senate frequently leans over and seeks advice from the parliamentarian. He then repeats that advice as a ruling of the chair. Occasionally the ruling has been carefully worked out in advance and in secret. Because parliamentary tactics often spell the difference between success and failure of an amendment or an entire bill, his rulings are crucial as they determine whether an amendment will be considered or a measure ruled out of order. The parliamentarian must therefore be above suspicion and above the fray of partisan politics. But this works only so long as the majority of the Senate agrees to play by the rules and does not fire the parliamentarian.[15]

Shortly before losing control of the Senate, Republican leaders of the 107th Congress (2001–2003) dismissed the parliamentarian because of their frustration over his rulings on tax and budget matters. "He's made inconsistent calls, and frustration has mounted," said one staff assistant. "He has made it hard for the leadership to plot a strategy."[16] One of the parliamentarian's rulings was that only one tax bill could be considered this year under special budget rules that prevent filibusters. The final straw came when the parliamentarian determined that a Republican plan to set aside more than $5 billion in the next year's budget to cover expenses related to natural disasters could be removed from the budget unless Republicans could muster sixty votes to keep it. This decision frustrated Republicans, since earlier he delighted Republicans and infuriated Democrats by declaring that a tax cut could be considered under procedures that prevent filibusters on measures that reduced budget deficits.

Senate leaders must fulfill their traditional role in managing the legislative business of the chamber, while simultaneously seeking to structure floor action to publicize partisan messages. In such a message-driven partisan environment, and without the cooperation of the minority leader, the traditional Senate practice of unanimous consent—essential to keeping legislative business flowing in a chamber with extremely loose rules for floor debate—has become much harder to achieve.[17] Herrnson and Patterson demonstrate the difficulties members and staff confront when trying to construct and communicate a partisan agenda. Meeting these is especially challenging when the individuals who assume primary responsibility for the agenda-setting process have few perks with which to encourage others to participate. Simply put, high-profile legislation rarely passes.

LEGISLATIVE BLITZKRIEG OR LEGISLATIVE LULLABY

Elections convey fresh messages that influence newly elected officials' behavior as well as that of incumbents. Elections also figure prominently into the agenda-setting process. Congress's agenda typically does not change incrementally. Instead, public policy shifts in major ways, or in a flurry, near an election for example. Several different developments seem to come together at once to produce these changes as people on Capitol Hill identify and focus on certain problems rather than others, and they propose and refine policy proposals for reasons other than actually solving problems.

Following the electoral earthquake of 1994—the Democrats' Pearl Harbor— the Republicans of the 104th Congress (1995–1997) arrived with a sense of purpose and the zeal of missionaries. "They came to town . . . sweeping all before them, the conquering heroes with a justified sense of satisfaction that they could truly change America," recalled Senator John McCain (R-Ariz.).[18] Once seated, Speaker Newt Gingrich (R-Ga.) and his lieutenants not only submitted their blueprint for battle but also outlined a strategy for fulfilling that plan. The initial battle plan was to reshape the procedural environment in which the House conducts business, reprioritizing policy issues.[19] New tactics and relationships emerged, bringing to the fore new political networks affecting participation and influence on policy and altering the distribution of influence. Lawmakers spent marathon sessions voting and filled the hours with contentious debate over the ethics of each other's leaders.

Following the next election and the Republicans' loss of House and Senate seats, the Republican-controlled 105th Congress (1997–1999) was quiet by comparison, going through what one observer called a "legislative lullaby."[20] After the recounts, and some runoff elections in Texas, Republicans still outnumbered Democrats by twenty-one (228–207), but with a smaller margin than the twenty-five they had two years earlier (230–205).[21] Though Democrats nearly shut out the Republicans in the Northeast, Republicans continued to make gains in the South. In the Senate the Republicans gained two seats (55–45), getting closer to the elusive number of sixty Senate seats required to invoke cloture. While the impact was greater than the number suggests—because ideologically the new Republican senators moved the Senate further to the right—Republicans were still five votes short of the sixty required to shut off Democratic filibusters. Congress does not routinely work at the frenetic pace of the "100 days" of the GOP House juggernaut. Policy revolutions can be taxing and difficult to sustain, given the institutionalization of certain norms—seniority, apprenticeship, and reciprocity— and an institution that is sequential, approaching solutions in small, discrete steps, building policy from the bottom up. Elaborate written rules and practices that govern the conduct of both the House and the Senate make it extremely difficult to consider legislation at rapid speed. Committees are often slow to organize themselves into subcommittees, set their agendas, and even outline broad themes, especially when one chamber is evenly divided, as the Senate was for part of the 107th Congress (2001–2003).

The 1998 elections, which resulted in a Democratic net gain of four seats in the House and Gingrich's retirement from the House, continued the return to a decentralized legislative process. Lawmakers in the 106th Congress (1999–2001) emphasized an even more traditional model of congressional power, crafting most legislation in committees, with congressional leaders forced to bargain with the president. Even the once aggressive reform-minded Class of 1994 tempered their conservatism with a desire to fashion laws through compromise and gain more legislative influence.[22] "I think the freshmen reflect what their constituents feel—a very different mood from the Class of 1994," said Representative Steve Kuykendall, a Republican who won an open Democratic seat in Los Angeles in 1998.[23] "Those freshmen were aflame with fervor of their convictions, ready to flex their ideological muscles but unwilling to compromise with colleagues who did not share their views."[24]

The 2000 elections produced an almost evenly divided 107th Congress, with a House majority party that began with only a seven-seat margin of control, and with the Senate initially tied for control, with each party controlling fifty seats. Although Republicans and Democrats pledged to work toward bipartisanship, in such closely divided chambers, any partisan defections can profoundly affect the outcome of issues, which especially applies to those in the center of the political spectrum like conservative Democrats and moderate to liberal Republicans. So when narrow majorities exist, Congress must construct winning coalitions in order to function. Leadership is forced to woo renegade factions in their own flock as well as seek defectors from the opposition in order to negotiate policy matters with the White House.

But majorities, writes one observer, are built in Congress, not elected to it.[25] They are transient and fluctuating; a new majority must be pieced together to deal with each major issue, because leaders and regulars who form them leave Congress, and because public recognition of salient political issues changes.[26] Congressional decisions reflect this, as various leaders—committee chairpersons and party leaders—broker the products of the legislative process to rally enough rank-and-file to get a majority, and then maintain these unified blocks at each step of the legislative process to work and vote together in pursuit of particular legislative goals.

When the 107th Congress convened, a majority of House members had been elected in the 1990s. High electoral turnovers in successive elections have made the chamber significantly younger and more junior than it was when the decade began. These elections followed an interlude of uncommonly low turnover (1984–1990) that brought only 162 newcomers to the House—an average of 9 percent per election, compared with the normal rate of 15 percent or more. Less familiar with the institution, culture, folkways, and history, younger members often shun the intra-party or bipartisan comity needed to grease the gears of the legislative process.

The contemporary Congress reflects the "permanent campaign" that has become a hallmark of contemporary national politics.[27] In his effort to delegitimize the then-Democratic majority, then-Republican Minority Leader Trent Lott declared "war" on what he considered a majority built on immoral back-room deals to lure Senator James M. Jeffords of Vermont away from the Republican Party.[28] "We must begin to wage the war today for the election in 2002," Lott claimed in what amounted to a parting grenade hurled at Senator Tom Daschle (D-S.D.). "We have a moral obligation to restore the integrity of our democracy, to restore by the democratic process what was changed in the shadows of back rooms in Washington. . . . This is a great and worthy struggle. The fight is on."[29] Lott, himself, would later resign his leadership position, at the start of the 108th Congress (2003–2005), after it became clear that his support among his colleagues had eroded in the wake of racially charged comments he made at retiring South Carolina Senator Strom Thurmond's 100th birthday party, namely that the country would be better off if Thurmond had won the presidential election in 1948. Thurmond ran as a Dixiecrat on a segregationist platform that year, winning several southern states including Lott's Mississippi.[30]

UNORTHODOX POLICYMAKING

Fingers are repeatedly pointed at Congress as a contributor to and creator of many problems in the policymaking process. As with most human choices, motivations and goals in the lawmaking process are an intricate mixture of the undisguised and the disguised, the noble and the coarse. And, to be certain, Congress is an institution that prefers caution, characterized by a web of rules, structures, routines, and traditions. These norms mark the boundaries of the legislative playing field and define the rules by which the game is played. But much of congressional action in the modern Congress takes place outside what, for decades, served as Congress's major battlegrounds. In the face of challenging governing circumstances, lawmakers are finding unorthodox ways to formulate policy, to keep the lawmaking process going.[31] The use of task forces that bypass the regular committees and of postcommittee adjustments, including the replacement of committee bills by substitute bills that the leadership takes to the House floor, are just two examples of creative tools that have been fashioned in response to different problems and opportunities. These changing patterns in congressional practice and procedure have worked to facilitate lawmaking. Leadership is afforded more flexibility in shaping the legislative process to suit the specific legislation at hand, in advancing policy agendas, and in accomplishing other goals. The contemporary process is comparable to climbing a tree with many branches: "If one route is blocked there is always another one can try."[32]

Leal's examination of the rancor and distrust over the 1999 congressional Juvenile Justice vote exemplified an unorthodox approach to lawmaking on

Capitol Hill. The vote demonstrates how the contemporary lawmaking process provides congressional actors with more choices and how the alternatives they choose lead to different legislative paths, highlighting the range and variability of the contemporary legislative process. Members of Congress bypass established rules and make more permanent changes in the way the institution traditionally operates in order to gain political advantage. Hardball tactics by the leader of one party to sabotage another party's initiatives, for example, frequently lead to reciprocal schemes to hold favored legislation hostage.

Despite successful legislative outcomes with unorthodox lawmaking, there are cautionary pitfalls associated with too much innovation and modification. Congressional government may or may not be committee government, as Woodrow Wilson held.[33] But much of Congress's deliberation takes place in the committee and subcommittee rooms of Capitol Hill, and when these traditional channels of lawmaking are manipulated or short-circuited, deliberation and the quality of legislation decline.

THE LEGISLATIVE WAY OF LIFE

The legislative way of life is an inch deep and a mile wide. The hours are long, the travel demands are inhuman, and the schedules are ever in flux. The typical legislative day commences with a 7:30 A.M. breakfast with one group of constituents and ends with an 8:00 P.M. dinner with another. In between, members rush around helter skelter from one subcommittee meeting to another or wash back and forth to the floor to vote on waves of legislation. There is the posing for mandatory photographs on the Capitol steps with two to ten groups during any given day, the responding to press inquiries, and the editing of replies written by staff in response to letters from constituents. Committee meetings often overlap with floor sessions, creating scheduling conflicts. Senators, as Rae and Leal remind us, tend to keep a slightly more elongated schedule in Washington, partly because they face reelection every six years (compared with two years in the House) and are under less pressure to spend every weekend tending to supporters at home. Like simultaneous forest fires each competing for a firefighter's attention, legislative, political, and fundraising considerations compete for a member's attention.[34] Members prioritize the issues that create the greatest pressure.

Congressional committees are "miniature legislatures" or "microcosms" of their parent bodies, subject to the same influences as their parent chambers.[35] Although the format and ground rules for congressional hearings vary by committee and response to specific circumstances, most are conducted with little fanfare. In general, witnesses give testimony from prepared statements while committee or subcommittee members occasionally follow along.

More often than not, members utilize this time to review their correspondence or consult with staff. When the testimony ends, a rotating cast of committee members ask questions in order of seniority, beginning with the chair, then the ranking minority member, and so on, alternating back and forth between the parties. Ordinarily time is restricted, making it unusual for very junior members—especially those in the House—to question witnesses. Committee interrogation, like cross-examination in a courtroom, is an art in itself. Effective interrogation is based upon clear understanding of the objectives to be achieved and a grasp of the basic facts that are involved in the matter at hand. Unfriendly interrogation begins with questions that demonstrate the incompetence or unreliability of the witness.

RECONCILING INHERENT DIFFERENCES

Amid the fast and furious game over valuable Senate real estate during the Senate's transition from Republican to Democratic control, another battle was quietly unfolding on the other side of the Capitol, where Ways and Means Chairman Bill Thomas (R-Calif.) angered committee Democrats by severely restricting their access to panel rooms, the hearing room (where panel aides had been able to escort tourists and VIPs) and to the committee's library.[36] Thomas's actions have made it more difficult for minority members and their aides to plan and conduct meetings. Because of these restrictions, Democrats have been forced to find other venues for gatherings, a difficult task when space (or lack thereof) is prime real estate on Capitol Hill. "Stuffing 15 people in a member's office? We don't have those kind of facilities," a Democratic staffer complained upon cramming more than a dozen members and aides into a lawmaker's personal office for a meeting because they could not get a committee room.[37]

An age-old conflict of representation is whether legislators should govern as instructed delegates and respond directly to their constituents, or govern as trustees and use their own judgment to take positions they deem responsible, even when their constituents disagree with them. Jeffrey Biggs's examination of how Speaker Thomas Foley (D-Wash.) lost his seat in the House of Representatives when he became entangled in the cross fire between term limit advocates at home in eastern Washington and his congressional colleagues on Capitol Hill illustrates this point. Departing from the modern norm, Foley chose responsibility over responsiveness on term limits, which subsequently cost him his long-held congressional seat. He followed the Burkean dictum that lawmakers should overcome parochial interests and accept a more independent role from their constituency, being unfettered to act in pursuit of welfare and national interests.

"They try to treat a political issue like a science," commented one Senate legislative director in reference to the two tax committees on Capitol Hill: the House Ways and Means Committee and the Senate Finance Committee.[38] Regardless, the institutional base for congressional tax policy is as old as Congress itself. Tax legislation must originate in the House of Representatives and then proceed to the Senate. The House's bill frequently exhibits the handiwork of powerful party leaders, committee members, and lobbyists who have access to these individuals. Members of the Senate are accustomed to following their own inclinations and responding to party leaders, other senators, and interest group representatives whose views they agree with, when crafting taxes. The result is that the two chambers can produce vastly different tax policies. Differences in constituencies, terms of office, and legislative procedures that exist between the two chambers provide some of the foundations for the chambers' distinctive products. Other differences stem from the partisan makeup of the two chambers and the ambitions of their members. Such variance sets the stage for the annual battle royal that takes place in the Conference Committee that seeks to reconcile the differences between the measures.

CONCLUSION

Collectively, the volume's essays have shown that Congress is a living, dynamic institution. Sometimes slowly, sometimes rapidly, congressional membership, organization, and procedures are constantly changing under the impact of the shifting economic, political, and social circumstances of the nation. Some fundamental features of the first branch of government have changed very little. The basic constitutional structure and powers of Congress have not been much altered since the House and Senate first convened in 1789. Congress's operations are still governed by rules and norms and by the skills and personalities of those who apply them and the conflicts they sometimes generate. Because Congress also moves at its own pace, meetings and votes are often moved up in the calendar, delayed, or laid to rest—and very rarely for reasons of scheduling alone.

What have changed are the conditions in the legislature. Razor-thin majorities in the House and the oscillating majorities in the Senate have made compromise more difficult. Many current members of Congress approach the legislative arena with a singular objective: unconditional victory. They are willing to sacrifice longstanding rules and precedents in order to achieve their short-term goals. The battle over judicial appointments is a useful example. Senate leaders in recent Congresses have sought to curb a particularly potent weapon against presidential nominations: the filibuster. Supporters of reform suggest that this dilatory device encourages a minority intent on obstructing the will of the majority, and reforming it will bring

LESSONS FROM THE BATTLEFIELD

an end to gridlock on judicial nominations. Critics point to the "advice and consent" role of the Senate, arguing that tinkering with this device will undermine the upper chamber's constitutional responsibility to render its judgment on presidential nominees, leading to intensified tensions within the chamber.[39] Neither side is interested in compromise. Without compromise, politics becomes more like warfare, and the interests of the people are less well-served.

NOTES

1. Tom Downey, "Tales from the House Gymnasium," in *Inside the House: Former Members Reveal How Congress Really Works*, ed. Lou Frey, Jr. and Michael T. Hayes (Lanham, MD: University Press of America, 2001), p. 45.
2. John J. Pitney, Jr., "War on the Floor," in *Congressional Parity: Where Do We Go from Here? Extension of Remarks*, ed. Burdett A. Loomis (Lawrence, KS: University of Kansas, 2001).
3. Bertram M. Gross, *The Legislative Struggle: A Study in Social Combat* (New York: McGraw-Hill, 1953), p. 4.
4. Pitney, Jr., "War on the Floor"; and Barbara Sinclair, *Legislators, Leaders and Lawmaking: The U.S. House of Representatives in the Postreform Era* (Rathmore: Johns Hopkins University Press, 1998).
5. Ibid.
6. Quoted in Michael Grunwald and Helen Dewar, "Strains Drive Hill Toward Gridlock: Parties Stress Difference, No Deals," *Washington Post*, 1 August 1999, A1.
7. Helen Dewar, "Flip Side in the Senate: Different Teams, Same Playbook," *Washington Post*, 25 June 2001, A13.
8. Roger H. Davidson, "The 2000 Elections: A New Gilded Age?" in *Congressional Parity: Where Do We Go from Here? Extension of Remarks*, ed. Burdett A. Loomis (Lawrence, KS: University of Kansas, 2001).
9. Pitney, Jr., "War on the Floor."
10. Quoted in Eric Schmitt, "Gephardt Uses Films to Inspire the Troops," *New York Times*, 29 June 2000, A24.
11. Quoted in Lloyd Grove and Beth Berselli, "The Reliable Source," *Washington Post*, 27 October 2000, C3.
12. Nicol C. Rae and Colton C. Campbell, "Party Politics in the Contemporary Senate," in *The Contentious Senate: Partisanship, Ideology, and the Myth of Cool Judgment*, ed. Colton C. Campbell and Nicol C. Rae (Lanham, MD: Rowman & Littlefield, 2001).
13. Quoted in Richard F. Fenno, Jr., "Senate," in *The Encyclopedia of the United States Congress*, vol. 4, ed. Donald C. Bacon, Roger H. Davidson, and Morton Keller (New York: Simon & Schuster, 1995), p. 1785.
14. James Madison, Federalist 62, in Alexander Hamilton, James Madison, and John Jay, *The Federalist Papers*, ed. Clinton Rossiter (New York: Mentor, 1961).
15. Jeffrey H. Smith, "Lott Rules—and Senate Rules Suffer," *Washington Post*, 12 May 2001, A25.
16. Quoted in David E. Rosenbaum, "Rules Keeper Is Dismissed by Senate, Official Says," *New York Times*, 8 May 2001, A20.
17. C. Lawrence Evans and Walter J. Oleszek, "Message Politics and Procedure Politics," in *The Contentious Senate: Partisanship, Ideology, and the Myth of Cool Judgment*, ed. Colton C. Campbell and Nicol C. Rae (Lanham, MD: Rowman & Littlefield, 2001).
18. Quoted in Dan Balz, "Subdued GOP Resumes Lead with Eye to Past; Party Retained Hold on Power, Lost Consensus on Agenda," *Washington Post*, 8 January 1997, A9.
19. James G. Gimpel, *Fulfilling the Contract: The First 100 Days* (Boston, MA: Allyn and Bacon, 1996); and James A. Thurber, "Remaking Congress after the Electoral Earthquake of 1994," in *Remaking Congress: Change and Stability in the 1990s*, ed. James A. Thurber and Roger H. Davidson (Washington, D.C.: CQ Press, 1995).
20. Guy Gugliotta, "In the Cradle of Republican Revolution, a Legislative Lullaby," *Washington Post*, 1 March 1997, A4.

21. The figures include Representative Bernard Sanders (I-Vt.). Sanders commonly voted with the Democratic Party in the 104th Congress. In the first session of the 105th Congress (1997–1999), after four vacancies, the Republican margin shifted to 228–203. Representative Walter Capps (D-Calif.) died, Representative Thomas M. Foglietta (D-Pa.) resigned, Representative Floyd H. Flake (D-NY) resigned, and Representative Sonny Bono (R-Calif.) died.
22. Nicol C. Rae, *Conservative Reformers: The Republican Freshmen and the Lessons of the 104th Congress* (Armonk, NY: M. E. Sharpe, 1998).
23. Quoted in David Broder, "A Kinder, Gentler House of Representatives," *Buffalo News*, 9 January 1999, 3C.
24. Ibid.
25. John F. Manley, "The Conservative Coalition in Congress," *American Behavioral Scientist* (1973): 224.
26. Alan L. Clem, "Blocs and Coalitions," in *The Encyclopedia of the United States Congress*, vol. 1, ed. Donald C. Bacon, Roger H. Davidson, and Morton Keller (New York: Simon & Schuster, 1995).
27. Norman Ornstein and Tomas E. Mann, eds., *The Permanent Campaign and Its Future* (Washington, D.C.: The AEI Press, 2000); and Davidson, "The 2000 Elections: A New Gilded Age?"
28. Quoted in Philip Shenon, "Lott Steps Aside, Making a Pledge of Cooperation," *New York Times*, 8 June 2001, A23.
29. Quoted in Paul Kane, "GOP Plays Hardball on Panel Resolution," *Roll Call*, 4 June 2001: 1.
30. Michael S. Gerber, "GOP Senators Elect Frist as Their Leader," *The Hill*, December 20, 2002.
31. Barbara Sinclair, *Unorthodox Lawmaking* (Washington, D.C.: CQ Press, 1997).
32. Ibid., p. 31.
33. Woodrow Wilson, *Congressional Government: A Study in American Politics*, 4th ed. (Boston, MA: Houghton, Mifflin and Company, 1887).
34. David S. Schuman, "A Space Enthusiast's Political Primer," *Ad Astra*, March/April 2001: 26.
35. Ralph K. Huitt, "The Congressional Committee: A Case Study," *American Political Science Review* 48 (1954): 340.
36. Ben Pershing, "Thomas, Democrats 'Locked' in Dispute," *Roll Call*, 18 June 2001: 1.
37. Ibid.
38. Authors' personal interview, legislative director for a western senator, December 15, 1999, Washington, D.C.
39. Author's observation, U.S. Senate, Committee on Rules and Administration, Hearing on Senate Rule XXII and Proposals to Amend this Rule, June 5, 2003, SR-301, Russel. Senate Office Building, Washington, D.C.

INDEX